RIGHT-SIZING YOUR LIFE

The Up Side
of Slowing Down

Philip D. Patterson &
Michael W. Herndon

InterVarsity Press
Downers Grove, Illinois

InterVarsity Press
P.O. Box 1400, Downers Grove, IL 60515
World Wide Web: www.ivpress.com
E-mail: mail@ivpress.com

InterVarsity Press® is the book-publishing division of InterVarsity Christian Fellowship/USA®, a student movement active on campus at hundreds of universities, colleges and schools of nursing in the United States of America, and a member movement of the International Fellowship of Evangelical Students. For information about local and regional activities, write Public Relations Dept., InterVarsity Christian Fellowship/USA, 6400 Schroeder Rd., P.O. Box 7895, Madison, WI 53707-7895.

Cover photograph: Peter Correz/Tony Stone Images

ISBN 0-8308-1942-8

Printed in the United States of America ♻

Library of Congress Cataloging-in-Publication Data

Patterson, Philip.
    Right-sizing your life: the up side of slowing down / Philip D.
Patterson, Michael W. Herndon.
        p. cm.
    Includes bibliographical references.
    ISBN 0-8308-1942-8 (paperback : alk. paper)
    1. Christian life.   2. Conduct of life.   I. Herndon, Michael W.
II. Title.
BV4501.2.P3545 1998
248.4—dc21
                                                                    98-6085
                                                                        CIP

20	19	18	17	16	15	14	13	12	11	10	9	8	7	6	5	4	3	2	1
15	14	13	12	11	10	09	08	07	06	05	04	03	02	01	00	99	98		

This book is dedicated to our families.
We would gladly die for them.
We hope that we will live for them as well.

Keep falsehood and lies far from me;
   give me neither poverty nor riches,
   but give me only my daily bread.
Otherwise, I may have too much and disown you
   and say, "Who is the LORD?"
Or I may become poor and steal,
   and so dishonor the name of my God.

Proverbs 30:8-9

If the devil can't make us bad, he will make us busy.

Corrie ten Boom

1

....

You May
Need to Right-Size
Your Life If . . .

You might want to think about making your life less complex if

☐ you have been to the doctor more than twice in the last year for a headache, stomachache, depression or anxiety

☐ you have difficulty falling asleep or staying asleep at night

☐ you have a hard time juggling bills and meeting your monthly budget

☐ you find it difficult to carve out time to attend church services

☐ you frequently get to the end of the day and realize that you have prayed only at mealtimes

☐ you have eaten six meals or fewer at home with your family in the past week

☐ you find that you spend fewer than fifteen minutes with each of your children individually per day

☐ you would be willing to give up 15 percent of your income

for more control over your working conditions

☐ you are often dissatisfied with the way you juggle the obligations you have toward family, friends, spiritual life and career

☐ you have given up a hobby, such as a fitness regimen or crafts, due to lack of time

☐ in the last six months you have been called out of a family event or social activity at least once for business purposes

☐ you or your spouse have added a part-time job in the past year in order to pay bills

Painful Sacrifices

The 1995 Oklahoma City bombing shattered not only the federal government building but also the community we live in. One of the doctors who helped in the rescue operation worships with us. He helped operate on the last victim brought out of the rubble alive—Daina Bradley.

Daina Bradley made the news because the doctors had to amputate her leg in order to remove her from the debris and save her life. But before they could perform that operation, they had to convince her that she would not survive with her leg intact. Her leg—so vital to her life earlier in the day—was now standing between her and life. She had to perform "mental surgery" on that limb before the doctors performed the actual amputation, realizing that it would be better to live without the leg than not to live at all. So after being trapped in the rubble for more than twelve hours and facing death if she kept the leg, she let it go.

This book is a call for all Christians to perform radical surgery on their lifestyles and live a life of simplicity. It is just as important for us to be free from the burden of debt and overwork in order to save our families as it was for Daina Bradley to be free of the weight of the collapsed building in order to save her life.

While not intending to trivialize her trauma, we believe that the decisions called for in this book can be nearly as painful and almost as radical for some readers as losing a leg was to Daina. However, just as the surgery was necessary for Daina to survive, your life might need a radical change if you are to survive spiritually.

There are things in our schedules that we don't want to let go any more than Daina wanted to let go of her leg. But we serve a Savior who told a rich young ruler to sell everything he had and follow God. He demands no less of us today. And while God may not be calling you to sell everything you have to serve him full time, he is calling each of us to put everything second after our relationship with him.

We do not present ourselves as being perfect in our priorities or in balancing the demands of our professions, our families and our Lord. However, we hope that we see our excesses and try constantly to improve. At one time each of us was working fifty to sixty hours a week, believing that the main thing our families needed from us was a healthy paycheck. And over time, with prayer and commitment, each of us has changed while still holding demanding jobs.

Our desire in writing this book is to encourage people who

are considering right-sizing their lives to do so. We hope to educate young people who have recently married and are thinking about buying that new house or bigger car. We would like them to consider the future ramifications of their options. To those further along in life we would like to show options and benefits to rolling back some of the decisions you might have already made.

Parents have a responsibility to teach their children to live a balanced life and to model that life as well. Most of us have good intentions and good hearts and would love to be more productive in sharing our lives, but we simply don't have time. We would love to devote more of our time to learning God's Word and God's principles for our lives, but we are simply too overcome by the pressures of keeping up with our frantic pace. This book is written to help you fulfill those good intentions.

We come to this project from two different perspectives— Mike is a medical doctor and Philip is a university professor. Each of us comes not as one who has perfected the juggling act required of all Christians today but as one who has recognized the problems of a loss of balance in his life and is trying to overcome them.

For Mike the wake-up call came when he looked at a picture of his son when he was three and realized that he couldn't remember much about that time in his son's life. For Philip it was when the last of his three children reached their teenage years and he saw that he was spending half his Sundays on the road speaking to other parents about parenting while his own opportunity to have a direct impact on his children's lives was slipping away.

This book is not merely an account of our journey toward spiritual sanity but a biblically based appeal for you to do the same and practical suggestions to help you meet your goals of a simpler, more reflective life.

Questions for Thought or Discussion

1. What is one thing you could cut out of your life that you wouldn't miss and that would free up time for other activities?

2. What, if anything, has been missing from your life so long that you no longer miss it?

3. Are you modeling the attitudes toward work and family that you want your children to have when they grow up?

4. If you've been given a wake-up call to seek a simpler life, what was it?

2

....

Living the
Balanced Life

A man unpacked his lunch and complained to his coworker:
"Bologna again! For the fourth straight day!"

"Why don't you tell your wife you're tired of bologna?"
asked the coworker.

"You don't understand," the man said. "I'm single. I pack
my lunches myself."

So it is with us. When we look at a schedule that's full of
bologna, isn't it true that we packed much of it ourselves?
"Many working families are both prisoners and architects of
the time bind in which they find themselves," states Arlie
Hochschild, author of *The Time Bind*. If our schedules are a
jail, then we are the jailer who holds the key to freedom.

Tad Bartimus remembers such a time in her life. She was
one of the most successful reporters of her generation until
she was crippled by both carpal tunnel syndrome and lupus.

She now teaches journalism, lectures to writers and reflects philosophically about her former globe-trotting, fast-paced life. She recently told a writer's workshop that we will be remembered as "The Generation That Tried to Do Too Much." Why? Maybe it is because as we juggle all our disparate parts what we are really seeking is connection with our own lives and with each other. We figure if we keep piling it on, acceptance and a feeling of belonging will follow. Sometimes we pile obligations so high that we are buried by them. A 1997 study by the Pew Research Center found that balancing hectic careers with family life is the number-one concern in most American families. Less than a third think they do it well, and less than half think they handle their schedules as well as their parents did.

Drop a frog into a pot of boiling water and it will hop out. But if you drop a frog into a pan of room-temperature water and turn up the heat, it will slowly boil to death. The same is true with us. We didn't get thrown into our hectic schedules all at once, or we would have likely jumped back in horror. We more likely slowly took on more and more responsibilities, never letting anything go as we added. Eventually we ended up crunched and had to steal time from other places—recreation, devotion, family life and hobbies.

The Myth of Quality Time

A summer 1997 *Newsweek* magazine stated what many parents had already discovered in a cover story entitled "The Myth of Quality Time: How We're Cheating Our Kids." Profiled in the story was an attorney who changed jobs in order to get more flexible hours. After years of struggling for more time with his daughter, he is now able to walk her to the bus each morning and have dinner with her each night. "These days are not replaceable," he says. "My children are different each day. That may be the myth of quality time—that time is interchangeable."

His sentiments are echoed by Anna Quindlen, who quit a job as a Pulitzer Prize-winning columnist for *The New York Times* so she could be home with her three children. She explained her decision in an article titled "Why I Quit."

My children were indeed behind this decision, as they have been behind literally every decision about the broad parameters of my life since the eldest was born a dozen years ago. They have given me perspective on the pursuit of joy and the passage of time. I miss too much when I am out of their orbit, and as they grow, like a time-lapse photograph that makes a flower out of a bud in scant minutes, I understand that I will have time to pursue a more frantic agenda when they have gone on to pursue their own.

In their 1995 book *Time for Life,* authors John Robinson and Geoffrey Godbey asked ten thousand people to keep minute-by-minute diaries of their activities. They found that mothers who work outside the home spend less than an hour a day in childcare activities such as feeding, bathing or reading to children, and that working fathers spend less than thirty minutes a day. They concluded that "being busy has become a status symbol."

As the amount of work we do increases, its role in our lives changes. In *The Time Bind: When Work Becomes Home and Home Becomes Work* author Arlie Hochschild claims that for many workers the roles of office and home have been reversed. Home is where parents work frantically to beat the clock and squeeze the most out of a limited amount of "quality time," while work is a place of companionship and relative freedom. Hochschild maintains that the myth of quality time has been a key factor in the hectic pace of most homes. "Instead of nine hours a day with a child, we declare ourselves capable of getting the same result with one, more intensely focused . . . quality hour."

As we speed up our lives, our children learn by example that the hectic life is the route to worldly success. In a *Newsweek* essay titled "Is This What Life's About?" sixteen-year-old Elizabeth Shaw describes her high-school life as she pursues entrance into a prestigious college.

My alarm starts to ring at 6:30 a.m. . . . I get dressed and gather my books together. When I'm lucky, I grab a quick breakfast before rushing out the door for my forty-five-minute commute. During the day I fly from one class to the next, using my spare time to finish my homework. . . . Once the school day is done, I'm off to a practice, club or volunteer organization. Sometimes these extracurricular activities are fun, but they always take a lot of time and effort. It's seven or eight o'clock before I get home at night. After twelve hours of running around, I still don't have time to unwind. I wolf down dinner, usually microwaved soup or cold cereal, by myself, as my family has already eaten.

Then I stagger off to complete my day with more studying.
. . . This cycle continues week after week, broken only by
weekends full of homework and chores.

In light of our hectic schedules, can "quality time" take the
place of the family time lost to our long-hour jobs? Probably
not, for several reasons.

First, as Stephen Covey points out in *The Seven Habits of
Highly Effective People,* "you simply can't think *efficiency* with
people. You think *effectiveness* with *people* and *efficiency* with
things. . . . I've tried to give ten minutes of 'quality time' to a
child or an employee to solve a problem, only to discover such
'efficiency' creates new problems and seldom resolves the
deepest concern."

Next, acquiring values requires time. Children need to be
around their parents in a variety of situations to begin to
understand the values that we are trying to teach, and there is
no way to shorten the process.

Third, many parents discovered that quality time takes
energy. At the end of a ten- to twelve-hour workday most
parents lack the energy or creativity to come up with anything
much more creative than a night in front of the television.
Consequently, many American families join the 35 percent of
the nation known as "constant television households," where
the TV never goes off as long as anyone is home.

Finally, quality time is unnatural at best and emotionally
unhealthy at worst. As Arlie Hochschild points out, "Quality
time at home becomes like an office appointment. One wouldn't
want to be caught goofing off."

Restoring the Balance

Christian lecturer Rick Warren says that our lives are composed of "grind time," "prime time" and "unwind time." Grind time is getting done what has to be done to make a living. Prime time is enjoying our family, devotions or time with friends. Unwind time is rest. Yet all too often we grind until we are exhausted. We bring work home. We wear pagers and answer them at home. Many of us are working eighteen-hour days without realizing it.

Serious distance runners know the dangers of constant grinding. They don't run their maximum number of miles each day. Instead they run long distance once a week, a "tempo" run once a week and an "interval" workout once a week. The rest of the days are filled with "junk miles" or easy days to allow the body to recover from the work of the day before and to prepare for the hard day ahead. If runners just run hard, their performance declines. In order to be at peak performance on race day, they incorporate rest days into the training scheme. The right balance between work and rest is essential to a peak performance.

The same is true with work. We cannot treat every day as a sprint without serious physical, emotional and even spiritual repercussions. But many of us have to sprint because of financial decisions that we have made, often many years earlier. Richard Swenson says that many of us live our lives without margin. A book without margins is unreadable; a life without margin is unlivable. He writes,

Marginless is being asked to carry a load five pounds heavier than you can lift; margin is a friend to carry the burden.

Marginless is not having the time to finish the book you're reading on stress; margin is having the time to read it twice.

Marginless is fatigue; margin is energy.

Marginless is red ink; margin is black ink.

Marginless is hurry; margin is calm.

Marginless is the disease of the 1990s. Margin is the cure.

The familiar passage in Ecclesiastes 3:1-8 is about a life lived with enough margin to enjoy it. It is not just a suggestion; it's a prescription for long life.

There is a time for everything,
and a season for every activity under heaven:
a time to be born and a time to die,
a time to plant and a time to uproot,
a time to kill and a time to heal,
a time to tear down and a time to build,
a time to weep and a time to laugh,
a time to mourn and a time to dance,
a time to scatter stones and a time to gather them,
a time to embrace and a time to refrain,
a time to search and a time to give up,
a time to keep and a time to throw away,
a time to tear and a time to mend,
a time to be silent and a time to speak,
a time to love and a time to hate,
a time for war and a time for peace.

The Teacher notes that a life that is all planting and no dancing is a life lived "under the sun," a phrase used repeatedly in Ecclesiastes 1 and 2. Life lived "under the sun" is "meaningless" and a "chasing after the wind." There is no end to labor and no satisfaction found in it.

But watch what happens to life when it is lived "under heaven" as Ecclesiastes 3:1 suggests. There is a time for everything! What happened? Did the day get longer? No. In Ecclesiastes 3 the measuring stick for a successful day changed: a good day is a balanced day, with enough time for every worthwhile activity under heaven, including leisure.

What's a "Perfect" Day?

USA Today determined that the average American would need forty-two hours in each day to accomplish everything that experts say is required of the well-rounded, health-conscious individual. This includes thirty minutes for exercise, forty-five minutes for personal grooming, two to four hours with the children and spouse, forty-five minutes to read the newspaper, one and a half hours commuting, seven to ten hours working, one to two hours on housekeeping and chores, fifty minutes for intimacy, plus time for such activities as cooking and eating dinner, indulging in a hobby, reading a book, listening to music and sleeping.

We need to change the definition of a "full" day. It is not a day in which we do a lot of one thing (for instance, work). A full day is a day in which we do several things in their rightful proportion. Diane Fassel, author of *Working Ourselves to Death,* holds seminars for workaholics who need balance in their lives. She sees workaholism as a downward spiral that begins with a loss of balance and ends with a loss of faith.

Spiritual bankruptcy is the final symptom of workaholism; it usually heralds a dead end. It means you have nothing left. I believe this aspect of workaholism is the most terrifying. It is frightening to be out of touch with a power greater than yourself.

When Mike and his wife, Jolynn, shared their decision to right-size with their accountant, he suggested that Mike work on Saturdays to increase his income so they could stay in the house they owned at the time.

Jolynn resisted, remembering early in my career when I had worked from 7 a.m. to 7 p.m. and a half-day on Saturday to bring home extra money and how tired I had become. We decided to quit looking for ways to stay in the house and sold it. Subsequently, we now maintain a better balance of rest and work and worship after selling the house and right-sizing.

For a lesson in balance, watch a graceful ballerina as she spins. Watch her head and her eyes. While her entire body is spinning rapidly, she holds her head still as long as she possibly can, fixing her eyes on a distant point. Then, at the last possible fraction of a second, she turns her head completely around and finds the point again. She is focusing on a single point to help her stay balanced even when everything else around her is spinning.

The same should be said of Christians. We're the ones who have a single distant point that is our entire focus—heaven.

And even when everything is spinning at an incredible pace around us, we must never lose sight of that focus. That is how to maintain balance in a hectic world.

Questions for Thought or Discussion

1. When you get buried by your work, who or what is usually to blame? You? The system? Debts or problems at home?

2. Once you identify the culprit, can you do anything about it?

3. How do you resolve the statement of Ecclesiastes 3 that "there is a time for everything" with the fact that few people seem to have enough time in a typical day?

4. Write down the activities you think should be a part of a "perfect" day. How many of them did you accomplish yesterday?

3

....

Packing Light for the Journey of Life

A call to the simple yet extraordinary life of faith permeates Scripture from the story of Abraham through the letters of Paul. While nowhere in Scripture is there an exact command for how successful a Christian ought to be, there are many indications that a Christian's success will be measured in a decidedly different way from the world's standards.

Christians are the fortunate ones who have read the end of the book and know the outcome. And knowing who will be the winners in the game of life affects how we keep score. That's what Peter indicates to his readers in his second epistle when he reminds them of how things will end and then challenges them to live their lives accordingly.

But the day of the Lord will come like a thief. The heavens will disappear with a roar; the elements will be destroyed by fire, and the earth and everything in it will be laid bare.

Since everything will be destroyed in this way, what kind of people ought you to be? You ought to live holy and godly lives as you look forward to the day of God and speed its coming. (2 Peter 3:10-12)

The passage indicates that since we know something the unsaved do not, we will behave in a way they do not. That's essentially what the command to be holy means—to be different—and it comes from the Greek *hagios,* "different." To live a holy life might mean that our career choices will be different from what they might have been. Our goals might be different. Our needs and wants might be different, our consumption patterns different. We will even treat our bodies—the temple of God (1 Cor 3:16-17)—differently as well.

Because we've peered into the future through the looking glass of the Bible, we are different people. That's why the Bible's seeming indifference to our earthly success is hardly surprising, despite the claims of some evangelists who preach a "gospel" of earthly success.

We'll start by looking at three arguments from the Scriptures for living a life of simplicity.

We're Taking Nothing with Us

Philip and his family once took thirty-five college students on a semester abroad program in Europe and learned a lesson in packing light.

Though we preached packing light to the students, some failed to listen and took several pounds of clothing that they scarcely wore. In addition, after three months abroad, most of the students were so overloaded with souvenirs that they literally couldn't take their clothing with them on the journey home.

In the end, we donated a lot of it to Croatian refugees whom we had been working with rather than take it home. That experience reinforced the fact that if we could begin to look at ourselves as sojourners rather than as permanent residents of this world, we would probably pack lighter— fewer obligations, fewer possessions, less overhead. But too many of us think we're permanent residents, and we get bogged down in the physical things rather than focusing on the spiritual. And in the end, like the clothing we left behind, we can't take all of life's baggage with us anyway.

In Mike's medical practice he has witnessed more than one hundred people draw their last breath as he tried to resuscitate them or while he attended to them as they died.

After each experience, after I have talked with the family and done the paperwork for the hospital and the funeral home has been called, I end up in my office or in the car alone. At that point, the thought always comes back to me that they took nothing out of this life. Many of them left behind a rich heritage for their children and maybe even an earthly fortune, but in the end, they left with no earthly possessions.

An interesting coincidence happened in our church in the fall of 1997. Just as the world was mourning the loss of Princess Diana, a member of our congregation, Bennie Warren, died at the age of sixty-five. Bennie had had such severe birth trauma that his parents were told he would not live, yet he did. For the first eighteen years of his life he suffered devastating seizures. By the time they stopped in his early adulthood, he was both physically and mentally handicapped.

But nothing slowed Bennie. He loved to sing and was in the worship service every Sunday. He was chaplain for a local civic club. He put pencils and attendance cards in the church auditorium for the more than fifteen hundred members who met there each week. He stood at the church door greeting everyone who entered there.

In some ways Bennie's life, which ended six days after Diana's, was quite ordinary. But in the ways that count, it was extraordinary. And though he was not famous and his funeral was not a state event, he left this world with exactly the same possessions that Diana did.

We are reminded several times throughout Scripture that we brought nothing into this world and will surely take nothing out. Shortly after Job had been informed by a series of messengers that his entire fortune and even his children had been taken from him, he uttered these profound words:

Naked I came from my mother's womb,
    and naked I will depart.
The LORD gave and the LORD has taken away;
    may the name of the Lord be praised. (Job 1:21)

That thought is repeated in Psalm 49:16-17.

Do not be overawed when a man grows rich,
    when the splendor of his house increases;
for he will take nothing with him when he dies,
    his splendor will not descend with him.

Even Solomon, one of the richest men the world has ever seen, repeats the same idea in Ecclesiastes 5:15.

> Naked a man comes from his mother's womb,
> and as he comes, so he departs.
> He takes nothing from his labor
> that he can carry in his hand.

Sometimes life teaches this to us before we die. Philip was once speaking at a church where the man who was to introduce him had left Philip's biographical information at home.

The man who was to introduce the lecture asked me to write down a few things for him to say. Minutes later his pager went off. It was his wife, who was still at home and had discovered his mistake. She began entering key facts about me to scroll across the pager. We laughed at her valiant effort to help, yet it was enlightening to find my life reduced to the 250-character capacity of the pager by someone who didn't know me.

Gone were the books written and the degrees earned, yet the names of my three children made the cut. Later it dawned on me that someday I'll have less than those 250 characters written about me on a tombstone. When my life is reduced to a few phrases, what will they be?

Riches Can Hinder Us on Our Journey

Have you ever packed too much for a trip, carried the baggage around for a week or more and, returning home, vowed never to make that mistake again? Seasoned travelers say that you will rarely regret packing too light, but you will never congratulate yourself on packing too much.

Hebrews 11 tells us that one thing all the great heroes of faith had in common is that "they admitted that they were aliens and strangers on earth" (v. 13) and looked for a city prepared for them by God. Are we living like we're on a journey, or do we look like permanent residents? Would anyone know our alien status if they visited our homes, followed us through a work week, looked at how we spend our money or saw where we invested our time?

We Christians must realize that each trinket we pick up along the way must be carried as we journey toward our final destination. Fine cars, boats and summer homes all pile up. And, ironically, after carrying this baggage throughout our life, we must leave it behind. If that is the fate of everything we accumulate, doesn't it make sense to travel light?

We're told in John that "the Word became flesh and made his dwelling among us" (1:14). The Greek word for "dwelt" implies not a permanent situation but a temporary arrangement. It could literally be translated "tabernacled" or, in more common language, "pitched a tent." The Son of God left heaven and pitched a tent here on this earth, at one point telling his followers that he didn't even have a place to lay his head (Mt 8:20).

How light are we traveling? How deeply staked is our tent? Could we follow the call of Jesus if he asked us to leave it behind to work in his kingdom? Could we scale it back a little to give our children a Christian education or help a missionary stay on the field? Could we forgo a promotion or a bonus incentive for the sake of our families and our own spiritual welfare? Or are we too heavily mortgaged and burdened with the luggage of this world to travel where the Holy Spirit leads us?

When Jesus claimed that it would be easier for a camel to pass through the eye of a needle than for a rich man to enter the kingdom of God (Mt 19:24), he had several reasons for the statement. First, he knew the tradeoffs and sacrifices that had to be made in order for a rich person's fortune to be accumulated. Sometimes the rich have set their priorities on earthly things rather than on the things above, which Paul urged the Colossians to seek (Col 3:1-3). Second, Jesus knew the attachment that fine things have on us. The more we accumulate in this life, the less we look to the future life for justice, reward or satisfaction. Jesus knew that the rich would become very self-sufficient, hardly recognizing their good fortune as a gift from God. That's the message of the parable of the rich fool in Luke 12, who congratulated himself on a good harvest and made plans to build even bigger barns. Jesus did not condemn the success; he condemned the man's attitude of self-reliance.

The writer of Proverbs puts it this way: "A faithful man will be richly blessed, but one eager to get rich will not go unpunished" (28:20). The act of getting rich doesn't have to actually occur for the punishment to be justified. You don't need to already have money to love money. It's the greed, not the riches, that is the sin, and greed is not just an affliction of the rich. It doesn't take an enormous amount of wealth for people to begin to love money and not be satisfied with what they have. Greed can easily tempt those who fail to be thankful for what they have and to learn to enjoy the lot that God has given them.

Ecclesiastes 5:10-11 describes how riches can consume the wealthy individual.

Whoever loves money never has money enough;
   whoever loves wealth is never satisfied with his income.
This too is meaningless.
As goods increase,
   so do those who consume them.
And what benefit are they to the owner
   except to feast his eyes on them?

Paul calls the desire to get rich a trap that many fall into.

People who want to get rich fall into temptation and a trap and into many foolish and harmful desires that plunge men into ruin and destruction. For the love of money is a root of all kinds of evil. Some people, eager for money, have wandered from the faith and pierced themselves with many griefs. (1 Tim 6:9-10)

Notice that it is the *love* of money that is the trap, not the money itself. It is the eagerness to get money, not the act of getting money, that leads some away. Those who are eager for money have "wandered from the faith." They've gotten lost on their journey, taking side trails that lead only to more baggage at the expense of reaching the eternal destination.

Greed can sometimes plunge generations of a family into unbelief. Proverbs 15:27 tells us that "a greedy man brings trouble to his family." He models bad behavior for his children, showing them a set of priorities that they will likely follow to their own folly later in life. Perhaps the greedy man takes illegal shortcuts, such as bribes, to accomplish his end, sending an even worse message to his family. A vast accumulated fortune, passed down for generations, rarely results in God-fearing children and grandchildren.

Philip teaches an ethics class each spring in which he asks each student—college seniors about to graduate—to write an essay about the most moral person they know.

I have never seen an essay that mentions wealth. Instead I see one essay after another mentioning sacrifice. And more than half of those essays are about a parent or grandparent. What a wonderful heritage to have a young adult child praise you not for your net worth but for your sacrifice. Perhaps that's what is meant in Proverbs 31:28, in the chapter on the wife of noble character, when the writer says, "Her children arise and call her blessed."

Moderation Can Help Us in Our Journey

If greed and the love of money are hindrances in our quest to live the holy and godly lives called for in Peter's epistle, then it is reasonable to assume that living a life of moderation in our desires and our consumption will benefit us on our journey. Scripture backs up this idea as well. We read in Ecclesiastes,

The sleep of a laborer is sweet,
    whether he eats little or much,
but the abundance of a rich man
    permits him no sleep. . . .

Then I realized that it is good and proper for a man to eat and drink, and to find satisfaction in his toilsome labor under the sun during the few days of life God has given him—for this is his lot. Moreover, when God gives any man wealth and possessions, and enables him to enjoy them, to accept his lot and be happy in his work—this is a gift of God. (5:12, 18-19)

What a contrast between the rich man and the laborer! Greed is replaced with satisfaction; sleeplessness is replaced with sweet sleep. A life that is meaningless becomes a life that is filled with joy. These benefits do not require a life of poverty, but rather a life of contentment. The man described here has enough food, enough wealth and possessions, and just as important, the right attitude toward his possessions that allows him to enjoy them.

The Gift of Enjoyment

A highly successful coach of the NFL's Buffalo Bills, Marv Levy, quit the coaching profession in January 1998 after leading his team to four Super Bowls in the decade of the 1990s. In leaving, he told reporters that the agony of losing had begun to far overshadow the joy of winning.

One does not have to have a high-profile job like Levy to understand. All too often the fruit of our labor spoils before we get to enjoy it.

Do you have the gift of enjoyment?

The gift of enjoyment allows us to be satisfied with the things we have and the things we accomplish rather than always comparing ourselves to someone who has more. It's a tough gift for many to ask for and even tougher to accept, for it means asking the Lord to work in us to roll back our worldly desires, but the benefits will be a happier, more satisfied life.

Philip spoke to his home congregation one Sunday, and a man in his early thirties waited patiently to talk to him after all the others had left.

For some reason the conversation shifted to accomplishments, and he made the statement "I'm not very successful in life." Earlier he had told me that he had just finished nursing school and was trying to support his family of four on his nursing salary.

In the weeks after we had our talk, I began to recognize his face in church. I noticed that he was always there with his entire family. Later, I noticed that he had his children in the same Christian school as my children, a significant sacrifice on his salary. Later I noticed he was actively involved in one of the church's ministries.

By every measure that I could think of, I saw him as a success, yet he saw himself as a failure. He was surrounded in the hospital every day by doctors making more in a couple of weeks than he makes in a year, and it was easy for him to apply the wrong measuring stick. But how many of those doctors were living for Christ? How many had happy family lives? How many had children being taught the Word of God daily at school and each Sunday in church? But his problem is widespread. It's easy to think we've failed if we use the measuring stick of the world.

Christian parents must model moderation for their children. Their peers are wearing designer clothes to school. Media messages are bombarding them, telling them that they must wear something, drive something or own something in order to be accepted. Nowhere is the message of sacrifice being taught to our children. By age eighteen an average teen will have seen 350,000 commercials, many of them aimed directly at adolescent insecurities by telling them that acceptance is only a purchase away.

James Garbarino, president of the Erikson Institute for Advanced Study in Child Development, summed up the problem parents face in an interview with *Newsweek*.

There is nothing new in greed, of course, but before there was television to inflame it, a child's frame of reference was limited to neighbors who were probably roughly in the same economic bracket. Now you're competing with the whole country, comparing yourself to people at the top of the ladder. People who didn't feel poor are forced to see themselves in that way.

Every parent must wrestle with the dilemma of wanting to do nice things for their children while at the same time getting them started on a life of sacrifice and satisfaction. And even after we have made the decision to live life in a simpler fashion, we must continue to reaffirm that decision or risk slipping back into a cycle of overspending and consuming.

The Gift of Appreciation
On three occasions Mike has gone on medical mission trips to Guatemala.

In the village where we worked, a researcher found that one gram of soil had over 150,000 worm eggs in it. In fact, I got scabies from holding infected children day after day.

At the end of the week, the team could be home within six hours, but home was really a world away in a community where the newspaper carrier makes more in a month than the average Guatemalan makes in a year. With each visit, two truths were reaffirmed to me. First, Americans are incredibly blessed. Second, my needs and my wants can get mixed up if I don't watch them.

On our last visit I took my daughter, Sada, who was twelve at the time. On the night before our departure we had spaghetti for supper, and Sada asked, "Are we having spaghetti again? I'm sick of it." My wife and I smiled, knowing what was ahead of her—several days of a steady diet of corn tortillas, black beans and rice. On the plane home she made the comment that some of Mom's spaghetti would sure taste good. She had learned early what many people never learn: that others get by on far less than we do and that many of our needs are actually only wants.

The plea of Proverbs 30:8-9 should be our daily request of God.

Keep falsehood and lies far from me;
> give me neither poverty nor riches,
> but give me only my daily bread.

Otherwise, I may have too much and disown you
> and say, "Who is the LORD?"

Or I may become poor and steal,
> and so dishonor the name of my God.

Aristotle advocated moderation, telling his followers to find the "golden mean." Often that mean is found between two vices. For example, Aristotle noted that courage is a virtue. Its deficiency is cowardice; its excess is foolhardiness. Lying between these two vices is the virtue of courage.

Each of us must find the golden mean for ourselves. Much of parenting is trying to find the mean between stifling our children's growth and letting them make too many mistakes from too much freedom. We must find the golden mean between earning a living and having family time and even between volunteering for good works and having family time. We must find the golden mean between denying our children too much and spoiling them. Moderation aids us in our quest for the holy and godly life that Peter commands us to live.

The Gift of Contentment

Paul tells Timothy that "godliness *with contentment* is great gain" (1 Tim 6:6). The two must go hand in hand. Where there is no contentment, eventually there will be no godliness as the discontented person begins to forsake the fruit of the Spirit (Gal 5:22) for the pleasures of the world.

Paul told the Philippians that he had "learned the secret of being content in any and every situation" (Phil 4:12). Consider the situations Paul describes in 2 Corinthians 6:4-5: troubles, hardships, distresses, beatings, imprisonments, riots, hard work, sleepless nights and hunger. Yet he could tell the Philippians that he had always found contentment no matter what the situation.

So what is the secret of contentment? Paul reveals it in Philippians 4:19 when he says, "My God will meet all your needs." Note that Paul does not say, "My God will meet all your desires." That is the secret of contentment that Paul learned and that we ourselves are still learning: to know the difference between needs and desires and to trust in God to supply our needs.

Questions for Thought or Discussion

1. What do you hope will be said about you at your funeral?

2. Why do you think the writer of Proverbs 28:20 condemned those who are eager to get rich rather than those who succeed in getting rich?

3. Do you agree that passing vast amounts of money on to our children could hinder them in their Christian walk? Why or why not?

4. How does a Christian avoid the world's "measuring sticks" for success?

5. The writer of Proverbs 30:8-9 pleads to be kept from both poverty and riches. What do you see as the spiritual dangers of poverty? Of riches?

4

....

Rest
Life's Neglected Third

In Time Shifting: Creating More Time to Enjoy Your Life *author* Stephan Rechtschaffen poses the question "Remember snow days?" He remembers them fondly.

As a child, when it snowed, I would get up in the morning and immediately turn on the radio to see if school was going to be closed—and how I rejoiced when it was! A free day, completely unplanned, in which I could do anything I wanted! It seemed like a present from God.

When I mention this in my classes, I can always see the recognition in the room. We sigh with nostalgia, remembering the unexpected pleasure of such days.

As adults, we need to create our own snow days, or at least snow time—a time for unplanned, unexpected events. We should offer this gift to ourselves. And why wait for snow?

In Mike's medical practice he has seen a interesting reaction when he pronounces a patient too ill or too injured to return to work.

It's as if I have pronounced a "snow day." It's almost as if they have to have my permission before they can take some time off. They are almost happy that their illness or injury has given them the time away.

But for every patient who is happy for their "snow day," there is one who is legitimately ill and needs bedrest and time to heal but refuses to rest. The price will be too high when he or she returns to work and finds a mountain of memos, e-mail and phone messages to answer thanks to the time off. What a shame that we're so bogged down that we can't even take the time to heal, much less relax.

What would it be like if the airlines treated their planes the way we sometimes treat our bodies? Imagine you're seated on a plane waiting to taxi away from the gate when the pilot announces, "Ladies and gentlemen, by the end of this trip this aircraft will have set a record for the most consecutive miles flown without stopping for routine maintenance." Would you be thrilled to be a part of aviation history or terrified that you might become an aviation statistic?

Systems analysts tell us that computers, those paradigms of efficiency, actually are inefficient when pushed toward the limits of capacity. In fact, some systems designers say maximum computer efficiency is achieved at about 30 percent capacity. After that, the computer can still take on more chores, but each additional task will be done with a little less efficiency than the previous one. Eventually, if enough tasks are added, the computer will crash. The most impersonal of inventions—the computer—shares this characteristic with humans. *Working longer produces more results, but not at maximum efficiency.*

The Jar Doesn't Have to Be Full

Perhaps you recall a science experiment in which the teacher took a jar and filled it with marbles and asked: Is the jar full? He or she then took pellets, poured them in the jar and asked: Is the jar full? Sand was added: Is the jar full? Water was added: Is the jar full? Even dye could be added to the solution when it looked as if nothing else could possibly fit between the cracks. It is often the same way with our lives: something can be found to fill every crack.

Psychologist Steven O'Brien is a strong believer in frequent, smaller vacations to match today's pace of life. "I think the once-a-year or twice-a-year vacation doesn't necessarily work for everybody," he said in an interview with the *St. Petersburg Times*. "You have to watch your expectations and not drill yourself into the ground with the preparations before you go."

"The real problem is the people who don't believe they can take vacations," says Eric Greenberg, director of the American Management Association. "They are running so fast to stay where they are that they are horrified that it will be worse when they get back," he said in a *St. Petersburg Times* article.

O'Brien seconds that thought. "Many of my clients feel guilty playing. They need to know that it's okay to go out and play. Sometimes workers have to stop and think: 'Wait a minute. Why am I getting on a guilt trip for taking care of myself?' It's like eating right. It's like exercising."

It's Naptime

Many of us would benefit from the old custom of taking a nap in the middle of the day. The word *nap* comes from the Old English word *knaeppin,* meaning "to sleep lightly." It is the way that 85 percent of all mammals rest, according to Claudio Stampi, author of *Why We Nap.* While our pet sleeps polyphasically, that is, several times a day, we tend to sleep monophasically, leaving us with what University of Pennsylvania sleep researcher David Dinges calls "the afternoon trough." According to an article in *Ambassador* magazine, Dinges says the trough is the time when we get the sleepiest, approximately twelve hours after the middle of last night's rest.

Both Stampi and Dinges as well as a vast majority of their colleagues agree that we would operate more efficiently if we gave into the urge and took a brief nap during the afternoon trough. Much of the world does this, and the practice is not limited to the Third World. The French and the Belgians spend an hour more each day sleeping than do their American counterparts. Even in work-crazed Japan companies provide rooms with tatami mats for a fifteen-minute afternoon nap. What companies lose in time they make up in increased productivity, claims Stampi.

But in America, Dinges notes, "time is for money, leisure or productivity, and anything else is viewed in a negative light, even though a twenty- or twenty-five-minute nap could increase efficiency." Taking that nap would put you in good company. Leonardo da Vinci took naps, as did Winston Churchill, Albert Einstein and presidents Coolidge, Kennedy and Reagan.

The personal and societal benefits of a short nap could be great. Studies show that we are more productive after a nap. We even have fewer automobile accidents after napping, according to David Willis, executive director of the Automobile Club of America's Foundation for Traffic Safety.

The same principle is true of exercise: if we make time for it we will find more time to do other things. In a survey for *Runner's World* magazine, the number-one excuse people made for not exercising was "not enough time in the day." Ironically, the number-one benefit that regular exercisers report from their exercise is that it makes the rest of the day seem less rushed.

Ann McGee-Cooper in *You Don't Have to Go Home From Work Exhausted!* compares the way we live our lives with the way a high-performance race car is driven—often resulting in the same situation.

Consider the Indianapolis 500, the major race car competition in the United States. Some of the most expensive cars in the world compete, most costing in the range of $600,000. Yet sometimes fewer than half of them are able to finish the race. That's a mere five hundred miles, a distance most cars in good repair could handle with no problem. Would you be willing to pay $600,000 for a vehicle that only had a fifty-fifty chance of traveling five hundred miles before breaking down?

So why are the performance records of these race cars so horrible? As compared with ordinary cars, these are built to run exclusively at top speeds. And for the vast majority of the five-hundred-mile race they run at only one speed—full throttle. All the other gears are used momentarily. It is rarely the super powerful engine that breaks down, but instead a minor part, such as a ten-dollar water hose or gasket.

We are so used to doing things at this accelerated pace that high gear is the only speed we feel comfortable in. And like the Indy cars, after a few months of operating at this speed, we experience small "mechanical failures." We begin to get headaches or sore throats, make careless errors, and have interrupted sleep. We also find ourselves stalled along the roadside by relatively insignificant obstacles, such as simple problems that we're too tired to solve.

In a world that is constantly threatening our ability to re-create ourselves, we must make an effort to relax and enjoy our God-given blessings. Following are four suggestions.

Find Your Plimsoll Mark and Honor It

In the late nineteenth century, some heavily loaded English merchant ships would sink under their own weight, resulting in loss of life and cargo. Compounding the problem was the fact that the ships were heavily insured against any losses, giving the owners little motivation to solve the problem.

Prompted by Samuel Plimsoll, the English Parliament enacted the Merchant Shipping Act of 1876. Among other things the act established a requirement that all merchant vessels have a load line painted on the hull that would be visible above the water only if the ship's weight was safe. The line became known as the Plimsoll mark.

Each of us has an internal Plimsoll mark, and each of us intuitively knows where our mark is. Rarely do the demands of our job alone take us to that mark. Those who are drowning in obligations are most likely driven there by the cumulative effect of jobs, parenting, church work, clubs and organizations. Others are drowning in debt, requiring them to take on second jobs.

Whether we are drowning in obligations or in debt or both, the secret to keeping our personal Plimsoll mark above the sinking level is *self-control*. When we say yes to serving on one more committee when our common sense and our calendar scream "No!" the line gets lower. When we join the growing numbers of people who won't take a vacation this year or a day off this week, we're loading our boats lower and lower.

Why not do a spring cleaning on your schedule and take out some obligations? And after doing that, don't add anything else without first dropping something. We are constantly asked to add another worthwhile obligation—chairing a school committee, coaching a soccer team, teaching a Bible class—without dropping any of the other balls we are juggling. Sooner or later what comes crashing down is our health.

Even good work needs to be subject to scrutiny. Diane Fassel relates that in her seminars on workaholism, she finds the most resistance from ministers, including one who blurted out, "It's not OK to kill myself for work but it is OK to kill myself for Christ."

Learn to Take a Trickle Charge

Laptop computers need recharging after about two and a half hours. There are two ways to recharge them. The first, and faster, is to turn it off and let it recharge. However, if the computer can't be spared that long, it can be plugged into the wall and charged as it's being used, which is called a "trickle charge." While doing the work it has to do, the computer is recharging itself for the next project. Often that is what we are forced to do in our daily lives.

Howard Thurman in his book *The Inward Journey* recommends "minute vacations" during the day. Minute vacations are chances to retreat from the present and put yourself into a less worried, less hectic posture and mental state, even if only for a minute. Ann McGee-Cooper calls these "joy breaks" from work essential. They can take the form of meditation, stretching exercises, calling a loved one on the phone or playing a computer game. Most managers think they can't enjoy anything until after their work is done. The trouble is, these days their work is *never* really done. So without any fun in their lives, they go into a state of exhaustion and depression.

Take Up God's Offer of Rest

A *Time* magazine article recently named America "The Land

of the Drowsy." Arlie Hochschild, in her research for *The Second Shift*, says,

> Many women I interviewed could not tear away from the topic of sleep. They talked about how much they could "get by on" . . . six and a half, seven, seven and a half, less, more. They talked about who they knew who needed more or less. Some apologized for how much sleep they needed—"I'm afraid I need eight hours of sleep"—as if eight was "too much."

In Isaiah 40:30-31 we are told that

> even youths grow tired and weary,
>
> > and young men stumble and fall;
>
> but those who hope in the LORD
>
> > will renew their strength.
>
> They will soar on wings like eagles;
>
> > they will run and not grow weary,
> >
> > they will walk and not be faint.

One of the indictments of Israel found in Isaiah is that the people did not take the rest that God offered them. In Isaiah 28:12 God says, "This is the resting place, let the weary rest," but the people would not listen. Later in that same chapter Isaiah condemns them for having made "a covenant with death" (v. 15).

Are we also guilty of this? Do we repeatedly pass up God's offer of a place to rest and run recklessly toward an early rendezvous with death? Can we even find God's resting place? David gives us a clue when he says, "I will lie down and sleep in peace, for you alone, O LORD, make me dwell in safety" (Ps 4:8). Our resting place is found in God. It's a relationship, not a location.

Perhaps one reason we hurry so much has little to do with economic necessity. Maybe we fear that if we become still we might have to meet God and come to grips with what our lives have become. As long as we're on the treadmill, we have no time for such painful introspection. But if things ever get still, we must face the God who wants an accounting of how we are spending his time.

God says to his people,

In repentance and rest is your salvation,

in quietness and trust is your strength,

but you would have none of it.

You said, "No, we will flee on horses."

Therefore you will flee!

You said, "We will ride off on swift horses."

Therefore your pursuers will be swift! (Is 30:15)

Even though Israel was surrounded by hostile nations, its salvation was not in its armies. Israel's salvation was contingent on turning back to God and accepting his rest. Yet they chose to flee on swift horses rather than accept those two conditions. They trusted in their horses rather than in their God.

In Matthew 11:28-30 Jesus makes this offer:

Come to me, all you who are weary and burdened, and I will give you rest. Take my yoke upon you and learn from me, for I am gentle and humble in heart, and you will find rest for your souls. For my yoke is easy and my burden is light.

What kinds of "swift horses" will we saddle and ride before we accept the simple offer of Jesus? For some it will be the swift horse of wealth. For others it will be fame. Some will take up his offer as soon as they have enough put away for retirement. Others will wait until their children are grown.

And what will we miss while we are riding our "swift horses"? A baby's first steps? A school play? Watching a son hit his first home run? Sending a daughter off on her first real date?

Seek Peace As You Would Any Other Worthwhile Goal

We often think of peace as a byproduct of something else. Early in adulthood we are tempted to think that peace is a byproduct of financial freedom. Later we think that peace comes from having faithful, fully grown children. Still later we look for peace in good health and freedom from illness. And after spending a lifetime of always thinking peace is only one more good fortune away, we find out too late that peace is not a byproduct of anything; it is an end in itself. Peace can be "caught" without catching anything else first. If peace were possible only through financial security or good health, God would have encouraged us to pursue wealth and health to get the peace that comes with them. But he told us to pursue peace instead.

Questions for Thought or Discussion

1. When have you felt the most burned out physically? Spiritually? Do the two coincide? What caused the burnout?

2. If your personal "Plimsoll mark" is below the water, how might you lighten your load?

3. What is it about running at a fast speed that is so attractive to so many people?

4. What are some ways of seeking peace?

5

....

Working to Live
or Living to Work?

In his short story "The Gift of the Magi," O. Henry tells of a poor young couple who had no money for Christmas gifts. The young husband sold his precious gold watch, without telling his wife, to buy a comb for her beautiful long hair. And without telling her husband of her plan, the wife cut her hair and sold it to buy a chain for his watch. Though they had good intentions, neither got a gift that could be used.

A similar irony has developed in today's household. Ask most parents why they work their long hours, and they reply that they work to provide nice things for their family. Ask children what they want most from their parents, and they reply, "More time." Neither side wins.

Often, however, the dynamics of the workplace work against the parent who wants more reasonable hours even at less pay in return for more time at home. Few jobs carry the security that was prevalent just a generation ago. In the April 1995 *American Demographics* magazine, editor Brad Edmondson captured the spirit of the age for baby boomers and baby busters when he asked, "Do You Have the Tickets?"

> It used to be a union card. Thirty years ago, that was a working man's ticket to a good job at a factory—a job good enough to pay for a house, a car, furniture, nice clothes and vacations . . . jobs that paid enough for their wives to stay at home. But then the economy changed and those tickets went away.
>
> Somewhere in the 1970s, the rules of admission to America's middle class changed. . . . The new ticket was education, but it wasn't a sure thing. That's why 60 percent of households now have incomes lower than $39,000, hardly enough to pay for middle-class existence—and to make that much, your spouse has to work.
>
> Today, you can find a ticket . . . in the chaotic house of a young lawyer and her computer programmer husband. He stops working at 3 p.m. to watch the kids and make dinner; she gets home around 7 p.m.
>
> Owning one of these tickets is the American Dream. . . . But no one hands you a ticket anymore the way a father once handed a union card to his son.

Times have changed in the American workplace. Few baby boomers will ever know the security of a single lifetime job. Few will have the experience of a single income covering the costs of owning a home and raising a family. No wonder that same issue of *American Demographics* declared that "no American is typical anymore. There is no average family, no ordinary worker, no everyday wage and no middle class as we knew it."

Not only are two incomes the norm for married couples with children, but a study released in May of 1995 by the Families and Work Institute found that women were the new providers of the 1990s. Researchers found that women were either an equal wage earner or the chief wage earner in 45 percent of all two-income families with children and 80 percent of all single-parent households with children.

Few of these jobs are flexible. Of the mothers who work, 65 percent have jobs requiring thirty-five hours or more weekly. And at least one 1997 study has shown that when companies do offer a downsized career track for those who want more time with their children, few employees—male or female—seek it.

Facing the Facts

Consider these facts, provided by the Child Care Action Campaign.

☐ In more than two-thirds of all two-parent families, both parents work. More than half of all mothers return to work or look for a job before their babies are a year old.

☐ Of the nation's twenty-two million children under age six, at least twelve million need daily care because their parents work.

☐ Children in "self-care" arrangements now number about seven million, and up to one-third of preschool children are thought to be left at home alone or with a sibling part of each day.

☐ There has been a 200 percent growth in single-parent households since 1970. As many as three-fourths of all children will live in a single-parent household before they reach the age of eighteen.

Economics drives the decision-making process in most households. Decisions made by the parents years earlier—educational loans, location of house, type of car, etc.—have ramifications years later when children enter the picture. At that point, parents have few options.

"Decisions aren't made on the basis of what's best for the child, but what can the child tolerate," says James Garbarino, president of the Erikson Institute for Advanced Study in Child Development. "With infants, it's how soon can they go to day care so the parents can go to work? With eight- or nine-year-olds, it's how soon can they come home alone? It's all designed to make the participation of adults in the work force easier."

This chapter is not an indictment of the two-income family, but parents need to realize that children today are being blindsided by a triple threat to their parental time: both parents usually work; one or both parents often have demanding, long-hour jobs; and a huge number of parents will divorce, leaving children fatherless or motherless. According to David Blankenhorn of the Institute for American Values, children can handle the first two situations far better than the last.

The moral rule is that you do not bring a child into this world without a mother or father devoted to that child's well being. Roles can and should shift. But the number and identity of the parents should remain the same.

The cavalier attitude of many baby boomers toward child rearing can be seen in a quote by actor and comedian Mark Cooper. "I grew up in a unique household because I had a mother and father there. I think that really steered me on the right path. It really saved me." Society has changed drastically in a single generation when it is newsworthy that a family stays together.

Even those who are not divorced from their spouses are often "divorced" from the lives of their children. Tom Peters, a widely respected business consultant and coauthor of *A Passion for Excellence,* spells out the dilemma.

We are frequently asked if it is possible to "have it all"—a full and satisfying personal life and a full and satisfying professional one. Our answer is: No. The price of excellence is time, energy, attention and focus, at the very same time that energy, attention and focus could have gone toward enjoying your daughter's soccer game. Excellence is a high-cost item. As David Ogilvy observed in *Confessions of an Advertising Man:* "If you prefer to spend all your spare time growing roses or playing with your children, I like you better, but do not complain that you are not being promoted fast enough."

Sadly, some parents even prefer it that way. In *The Time Bind* Arlie Hochschild says that given the frantic nature of home life, the office has become the refuge from home rather than the reverse, as was the case a generation ago. Writing specifically about women's work habits, Hochschild says, "Women discovered men's secret. They discovered the appeal of work." Hochschild adds that parents today have "emotionally downsized" their lives to convince themselves that their children simply don't need as much attention as they do. They come to believe that a birthday party organized by professionals is superior to one they might do themselves or that a cassette tape at bedtime is as good as a parent reading a bedtime story. She concludes: "We need to look at the effect of the time bind on our lives and our kids' lives. Let's look in the mirror. We're complicit. Then let's get on to solutions."

Why Don't We Know Our Kids?

Born between 1964 and 1984, just after the baby boomers, the most heralded generation in history, is Generation X, named after that unknown mathematical quantity, x. In many ways, Generation Xers resemble the survivors of a holocaust. By some estimates, one-third of the generation was aborted before birth. And the survivors weren't very well cared for after birth. Their parents are the most divorced group in history. A Generation Xer has a 75 percent chance of spending some time in a one-parent household. Twenty-five percent began life that way; the others lost a parent to divorce or death later in life. Their parents work more hours than any parents in history, meaning that about a quarter of them come home from school to an empty house where they hook up with "electronic parents" such as TV, VCRs and the Internet. When they get into trouble, who's to blame: the kids, the parents, the media or the system of earn and spend that created the environment?

Some believe the trend can be reversed. In a *Fortune* magazine article titled "Is Your Company Asking Too Much?" author Brian O'Reilly notes that "it used to be that sixty-hour work weeks gave you warrior status, but the trend is reversing. People are now saying that sixty-hour weeks mean that something is wrong with the system or with the person."

Mike's family has a tradition that on his children's birthdays, he takes them out for a one-on-one date to eat and go to a movie.

After the movie we have a secret spot where we go and visit and say a concluding prayer after our evening together. A few years back I read a story that prompted me to tell my children how much I loved them. I told them that I loved them enough that I would die right now for them. It was not long after this that I was struck with a very sobering fact: the lifestyle that I was living was showing them that even though I was willing to die for them, I was not willing to live for them.

My new conviction to put my children before my job led me to look at our lifestyle in new ways. As a family, we had enjoyed going to church camp together. However, for the last two summers I felt we simply couldn't afford to miss a week's work to go to church camp and still take a family vacation. My focus was so much on providing things for my family—a large home, fine cars, expensive clothing—that I was missing out on being with them. Since I have made some changes in my work schedule, we have been able to go back to camp.

Right-Sizing: A Prescription for Health

Doctors hear and see many complaints and illnesses related to stress and burnout each day. One of the most frequent symptoms is headaches, but probably just as common is fatigue, as well as abdominal pain. Over the past few years more and more people have been coming to my (Mike's) office with symptoms such as these. Whatever the complaint, I find myself constantly making recommendations to my patients on how to improve their health, yet after I make these recommendations, the reply is often the same: "I just don't have the time to do that." Another common reply is "I'm just too busy" or "I'm too tired to get that done." Patients frequently ask, "Just how do you suggest I make time for that when I've got such-and-such to get done every day?"

I constantly stress a "lifestyle change" to my patients, a prescription that is not always simple. We must restructure, redesign and many times right-size our lifestyles in order to take control of our physical, emotional and spiritual health. And this change comes with some costs.

For example, it is not easy to turn down invitations that carry prestige. Two years ago I was asked to serve on the state medical association board. I truly wanted to do this, but after consulting with my wife, I knew this was the wrong thing for me to do at this stage in my career. I have been asked several times to serve on the boards of charitable organizations and have turned these opportunities down as well.

I also faced the cost of leaving the fine home that we were in and moving to something smaller with fewer amenities. I chose to drive Fords instead of a Cadillac and a Lexus. And I have to explain to peers that the things we gave up just weren't worth the price. The bottom line is that they are not as important as my family and my relationships with friends and with God.

Giving the Gift of Time

A recent TV commercial depicts an excited employee saying, "There is no nine to five here. It's get the laptop out and go twenty-four hours a day." The smiling employee says that she likes her job because making customers happy makes her happy.

Nowhere in this upbeat commercial is the effect of that attitude shown. No lonesome spouses. No empty chairs at dinner. No children who can't stay awake long enough for Mom or Dad to come home. That would spoil the image of an employee who puts his or her job before all other obligations and is happier pleasing customers than pleasing family members. And that's the image that most companies want to project: a group of happy, long-hour workers whose coworkers have become their surrogate family.

Columnist George Will says that "time is congealed money." Just as a large ice cube melts into a large puddle, those workers who offer their employers more time will usually see it melt down into more money. But when it is earned, will they have anyone to enjoy it with? Rosabeth Moss Kanter in *When Giants Learn to Dance* asked successful executives what their accomplishments had cost them. Their answers almost always included "gaining weight, getting a divorce, getting in trouble with the family."

Surveys show that total contact time between parents and children has dropped 40 percent over the past thirty years. And even the nature of that time has changed. Fathers are far more likely to show up at a concert or a Little League game—a prescheduled activity planned and coordinated by someone else—than to be at home when children are "offstage, unable to get started on something, discouraged or confused," Hochschild writes.

In one study researchers found that the average child received only eight minutes of uninterrupted solo time with her father daily and only eleven minutes with her mother. Author Josh McDowell, in trying to replicate that study in Christian homes, found that the average time a church-attending father spent with his child was actually *lower.*

At a time when vacations, meal times and other family activities are declining, Christian parents must remember that the "law of the harvest" rules in our lives. We will reap what we sow. And for a group of people who believe that, Christians seem to be doing very little sowing in terms of parenting yet naively hope to reap God-fearing children. Is it any wonder that many evangelical groups report losses of up to fifty percent of the children reared in their churches?

Any parent can relate to the end of Thornton Wilder's play *Our Town.* It's a play within a play, directed by the ever-present stage manager. In the last act Emily, who has died in childbirth in her twenties, asks the stage manager if she can go back and relive a single day. He reluctantly consents.

Back among the living, Emily relives the day knowing that she will die in less than fourteen years. Her parents, however, live the day precisely as they did before. When she tries to hug them longer, they shrug her off. When she is talkative, they are busy. After Emily stays among the living for only a few minutes, she tearfully asks the stage manager to take her away again. The indifference her living mother and father showed toward the preciousness of life is too much for her to take. From her perspective she can see how little they appreciated the gift of life.

"Does anyone realize life while they're living it?" she asks the stage manager as she makes her way back to the cemetery. "Only a few," he replies. "Saints and a few poets."

May God give us the vision of saints and poets so that we will realize that every day is a special gift from God. No day is insignificant, and no day can be lived again.

Questions for Thought or Discussion

1. If you could go back several years and reverse a financial or career decision you made, what would it be? Based on this experience, what advice would you give young married couples?

2. Well-known author Tom Peters claims that it is impossible to have it all, in terms of business success and a satisfying personal life. How would you answer that claim?

3. Do you know someone who does a good job of "realizing life while they're living it"? How might you develop the skill?

6

....

Downshifting for Life's Curves

Onetime presidential candidate George McGovern, seventy-three at the time, said in his 1996 book, *Terry: My Daughter's Life-and-Death Struggle with Alcoholism,* that he has only had two regrets in life. One was that he never made it to the White House, having been soundly defeated by Richard Nixon in 1972. The second regret was that he couldn't save his alcoholic daughter, Teresa. In 1994 she was found frozen to death in a snowbank where she had collapsed in a drunken stupor.

After Terry died McGovern pored over her diaries, contacted her friends and interviewed the many medical professionals who had tried to help her. He found out from the diaries that he had not been the father he thought he was. While he was spending eighteen-hour days fighting for his political causes, his daughter was writing in her diary that she missed her dad and that he probably didn't care about her anyway.

His message to parents is to carve out time for more happy interludes and loving moments with adolescent children when they're young and need you, no matter what the cost to your career. That way, he said, neither of you will have regrets. "I'd give everything I have—and I mean everything—for one more afternoon with her, just to tell her how much I loved her and to have one of those wonderful happy times we used to have too infrequently."

The question for us is not *whether* we will ever regret a furiously paced life, but *when.* For some, like George McGovern, it will come at the physical or spiritual loss of a child. For others it will come with an early heart attack or a broken marriage. Every person will eventually downshift. It's a natural process known as death. Unfortunately, because some people insist on living life at full gear until that time, they actually hasten the day when the ultimate downshifting occurs.

There are others, however, who know that life can be lived at a less frenzied pace. Called "downshifters," these are people who voluntarily step off the fast career track, opting for a slower or in some cases a regressive career track in exchange for more freedom. In *Downshifting,* author Amy Saltzman identifies five types of people who leave the fast track in exchange for a higher quality of life.

The *plateauer* . . . finds a job within a comfortable zone of pay and responsibilities and chooses to stay there rather than accept promotions that come with relocations and higher time demands. The plateauer may be someone who has taken advantage of a "parenting track" at certain corporations, opting for job security and less pay in return for fewer promotions and the demands that go with them. The plateauer is not a lazy person, but a person who has found a quality of life within a certain level of achievement and stays there, often for two decades or more.

The *back tracker* . . . actually moves back down the career ladder in search of that niche that provides a comfortable level of income with a maximum amount of freedom. Quite often the back tracker accomplished a lot early—several promotions, bigger offices with bigger staffs. Eventually, this person wants to exchange some of that income for more time, quite often when children start to grow up.

The *career shifter* . . . finds a less stressful career, often shifting from management to team member, from owner to employee or even changes jobs. They may even go from white collar professional to blue collar employee to get more freedom. These people are looking for careers more conducive to raising families or being physically healthy. They often leave high paying, high stress jobs for jobs with less stress, but more intangible rewards.

The *self employee* . . . finds greater freedom in working for themselves. In a survey of some three thousand new business owners, 54 percent said having "greater control over their life" was among the most important reasons for opening their own business. Thirty-two percent placed being able to "live where and how I like" at the top of their list. These people quite often work long hours, but they enjoy the freedom that comes with ownership. Quite often the self employee finds a way to make the business a family affair, involving children and parents alike.

The *urban escapee* . . . joins the growing number of individuals emigrating from large cities to do their work in areas more conducive to rearing children and relaxing. These are not commuters, they are residents of rural areas who either find employment in those communities or use technologies such as modems and fax machines or the Internet to link to their work in metropolitan communities.

To Saltzman's list we would add the following options as well:

□ The *flexi-worker,* who has found a way to work hours that are perhaps nontraditional or irregular but more conducive to juggling the responsibilities of parenting, being a spouse or serving the church. These people have put into action what 90 percent of all workers claim they would like: more flexibility for less pay.

□ The *permanent temp,* who likes to work only occasionally to help make ends meet or to earn money for a special family need, but otherwise remains at home. These workers are frequently found substitute teaching or working as temporary office help. Many work three to four days a week but like the control that being a temporary employee gives them regarding where and how often they work.

Often those who choose to downshift are misunderstood by their peers. Anna Quindlen, discussed in chapter two, won the Pulitzer Prize while writing an opinion column for *The New York Times.* Less than five years after winning her profession's top prize, she quit to devote more time to her family and to pursue her dream to be a novelist. A year after she left the

Times she wrote of the reactions to the move.

The reaction to my decision reinforced a sense I had always had that for women, life is a circle; for men it is a straight line. The guys seemed to have the idea that a career was inevitably a ladder. . . . Why in the world, many seemed to imply, would anyone pass on the chance to take the next rung?

When Life Gets Your Attention

Well-known personalities are not strangers to the balancing act of family and career obligations. In an interview with *Parade* magazine in 1996, Mandy Patinkin spoke of walking away from his role on a TV series that had won him an Emmy award. "I'm very glad to have that Emmy, but it doesn't remind me of a great year of work. It reminds me of the struggle my family went through. It's a medal for the decision we made." Patinkin walked away from his role on the popular *Chicago Hope* when he realized that he couldn't move his adolescent children to Los Angeles. He was gone for long periods of time, and even when he was home he was not available for his family. "I've always said that family comes first, but actions speak louder than words."

Tad Bartimus, also mentioned in chapter two, was an unwilling downshifter who now looks back on her former lifestyle in amazement. By the age of forty, Tad had stood at the top of her profession, but she had to quit when she was diagnosed with both lupus and incurable carpal tunnel syndrome. She now looks at many of her colleagues in a different light.

I want to say "Is it worth it?" to a friend who spends eighty hours a week at the office. This chic, intelligent woman who hasn't had a date in two years because she hasn't got the time, recently bought a high six figure home so she could entertain for business with catered dinners. She saw no irony in hiring a decorator to dress up a house where nobody's home, to gussy up a family room where the only thing missing is the family.

Can we really have it all? Will we want it once we get it? And who will pay for a success measured in job titles and merit raises? Will it be the people we love the most? The ones to whom we give what's left over after our jobs take the best out of us?

Sue Shellenbarger of *The Wall Street Journal* tells of a friend who left a frustrating executive position to become a self-employed real estate manager. She worked hard but was happier than at any time in her recent past. One special reward was that her child began doing better in preschool. Her five-year-old daughter had been miserable during her first hour at school each day and withdrew from the other kids. After her mother's job change, however, she went skipping into school and jumped into the activities. She was happy because Mom was happy, Shellenbarger reported.

More than 50 percent of all mothers with children are now in the work force. If both parents are equally busy, does quality time suffice? Research indicates that it doesn't. A study by Josh McDowell found that there was a direct correlation between the amount of a child's interaction with his or her dad and such factors as virginity and abstinence from drugs. No other single factor was as important as the amount of time spent between fathers and children.

This does not mean that one spouse must quit a job in order for the parents to have God-fearing children. It simply means that as the work hours of each parent increase and the contact time with children decreases, the odds decrease of children staying out of trouble and developing a faith of their own, and parents must seek ways to keep those odds in their favor.

The Three A's of Parenting

Researchers David Lewis, Carley Dodd and Darryl Tippens (see *The Gospel According to Generation X*) asked fourteen hundred teens from conservative religious backgrounds how much "focused interaction" they had per week with their father. Twenty-two percent reported spending less than fifteen minutes per week in one-on-one, uninterrupted time with their father. This group that spent little time with their fathers was found to be two to three times higher in rates of sexual activity and drug and alcohol use than their peers who spent greater amounts of time with their fathers. This group also was less committed to church activities and spiritual formation.

The researchers found that as time with the father went up, bad behaviors went down and spiritual activity went up. This led them to promote the "three A's" of parenting—availability, approachability and askability.

Availability can't be rushed and often goes unnoticed. Availability does not mean constant communication and contact; it means constant *opportunity* for such contact to occur. The apostle Paul became "all things to all men so that by all possible means [he] might save some" (1 Cor 9:22). We must become "all things" to our children—parent, adviser, confidant, friend—in the hopes that in one role or another we might make a difference in their lives.

But availability does not mean overindulgence. Even though we should be available to our children, our lives should not revolve around making them happy. Trying to make children happy all of the time is very unhealthy and creates dysfunctional people.

After availability comes *approachability.* "Are you busy?" is not a yes-or-no question; it's a plea for time and sometimes even for help. If you're sitting at your computer or desk or even just reading the paper, try this reply to the question "Are you busy?": "Not too busy for you." It signals not only your availability but also your willingness to get the dialogue started.

Finally, *askability* is a trait that must be earned. Who is the most "askable" parent in your house? Why? Can the less askable person (usually the father) take lessons? Fathers must do what they can to remove the natural barriers of asking Dad about life, sex, spirituality—all the big questions. Following are a few of the rules about "askability" from Lewis, Dodd and Tippens.

1. There are no dumb questions and should be no flippant answers.

2. There is no wrong time for an important question.

3. Act as if there is no other parent, even in a two-parent household.

4. If you have to, ask first. Your child may be "dying to

tell"—metaphorically or literally.

We do not have to make a heroic effort to have an impact on the lives of our children, yet all too often we settle for doing nothing. Irving Kristol of the American Enterprise Institute describes his simple relationship with his father.

As the son of immigrant parents, my father never did any of the things that according to the "parenting" wisdom of today are supposed to be so important. . . . He was always calm and genial and thought by all to be wise and fair and good. I thought so, too. He was, and remains in memory, a version of the good father. And I never felt the need for a better one.

Do something big, do something small, but do *something* for your children today.

Questions for Thought or Discussion

1. How can parents avoid the regret expressed in George McGovern's story?

2. Would any of the types of "downshifting" work for the wage earner or earners in your family?

3. What do you see as the biggest obstacle to downshifting in your life? What would be the greatest benefit? Is the benefit worth overcoming the obstacle?

4. Of the three A's of parenting—availability, approachability and askability—where do you excel? Which, if any, do you need to work on?

7

....

The Complex Problem of Simplicity

Simplicity is never simple. No matter how simple that perfect golf swing or flawless piano concerto looks to the casual observer, it is the result of much careful preparation and execution. The truly great ones make the difficult look effortless because they have practiced. The same is true with the simply lived life. It doesn't just happen that some people have lives that appear as easy as a well-played concerto. Things that are worthwhile are worth working for and sacrificing for.

The move to a simpler life is not only a good idea, but it's a biblical mandate for the Christian. In writing to the Thessalonians, Paul says, "Make it your ambition to lead a quiet life." In the next verse he explains why: "so that your daily life may win the respect of outsiders and so that you will not be dependent on anybody" (1 Thess 4:11-12). Live simply, Paul says, and the hustling world will notice and respect you for it.

Live simply and you won't be so burdened with debt or work that you neglect leading the type of life pleasing to God.

Vernard Eller in his book *The Simple Life: The Christian Stance Toward Possessions* discusses the meaning behind Jesus' statement in Luke 9:62, "No one who puts his hand to the plow and looks back is fit for service in the kingdom of God."

It is abundantly clear, first of all, that Jesus demanded as an exclusive priority that a person center his life, loyalty and valuations solely upon God. It is clear, in the second place, that his understanding of the simple life devolves entirely from this premise. Thus the doctrine of the simple life is indeed simplicity itself and can be very simply put: one is living the simple life when his ultimate loyalty is directed solely to God and when, in consequence, he lets every other concern flow out of, fall in behind, and witness to this one. . . . The simple life is not to be equated with the least possible consumption of worldly goods and satisfactions. No, the point is that these things can be good—very good—if they are used to support a man's relationship to God rather than compete with it.

If your life is complicated, you will have to uncomplicate it before you can reclaim control over it. Here are four methods to prioritize your life in order to begin to separate the trivial from the important.

1. The deathbed priority test. Louise Lague, in *The Working Mom's Book of Hints, Tips and Everyday Wisdom,* suggests asking yourself, "On your deathbed, will you wish you'd spent more prime weekend hours grocery shopping or walking in the woods with your kids?" The same goes for overtime, promotions that bring more responsibilities, and even volunteer work. Who, on their deathbed, will wish they had served on more church committees and spent fewer Sunday afternoons at home with their families?

2. *The disaster test.* A second test of priorities comes from Stephanie Culp's *Streamlining Your Life: A Five Point Plan for Uncomplicated Living.* Her disaster test is applicable to those who have trouble letting go of material goods. "If an earthquake, fire, flood or other natural disaster were to strike your life tomorrow, could you get by without the item in question?"

Sooner or later our possessions end up possessing us. Amy Dacyczyn, former editor of *The Tightwad Gazette,* frequently told her readers, "Every time you buy something, you give up a piece of your freedom." Vicki Robin, coauthor of *Your Money or Your Life,* lives voluntarily on seven thousand dollars a year. She admits to being "overwhelmed" by the demand for her book, which sold more than 300,000 copies, but is not surprised that growing numbers of Americans want to reclaim the American Dream from the grip of materialism.

In a nation where union leader Samuel Gompers once had a one-word reply to what the American worker wanted—"More"—it is refreshing to see that one-third of Americans told the Gallup pollsters in 1992 that they would take a 20 percent cut in pay if they or their spouse could work fewer hours. A 1995 Merck Foundation poll found that 28 percent of the respondents had voluntarily made changes in the last five years that resulted in their making less money. In the same survey, 72 percent of men and 87 percent of women said they wanted to spend more time caring for their children.

Juliet Schor, author of *The Overworked American*, says that more people are analyzing their lives and making changes. "For a lot of people, the system isn't working anymore. They're deciding it just isn't worth it. Why not opt out and build a sane life of your own?"

3. *The what-if-this-didn't-exist test.* A third test of priorities comes from *Stephanie Winston's Best Organizing Tips*. When going through mounds of paperwork and details, ask yourself: "What is the worst thing that could happen if this piece of paper didn't exist?" If the answer is "nothing," Winston suggests tossing it. Winston and her husband once went through their three-thousand-square-foot house eliminating what they hadn't used in a year. The result was a move to a six-hundred-square-foot condominium and a simpler life.

The test can be applied to housework, yardwork and other things that clutter our lives. Modify the question a little and ask: "What's the worst thing that could happen if this surface isn't scrubbed today or this closet isn't cleaned out today or the grass around the fence isn't trimmed this week?" If the answer isn't a fire hazard or ill will with your neighbors, eliminate it and—this is important—guard the time you save.

In times of war, army hospitals close to the front lines are forced to perform triage on the masses of wounded that come in all at once. The term *triage* is French for "prioritizing" or "picking out." On the battlefield, those performing the triage separate the wounded into three groups: those who will die even with medical attention, those who can be saved with immediate medical care, and those will survive even without immediate attention. It is to the middle group that the surgeons turn their initial efforts.

As Christians, we must constantly perform triage on our schedules, our obligations and even our volunteer work to make sure we are concentrating our efforts where they will do the most good.

Do you remember the story of Jesus at Martha and Mary's home? While Mary sat at the feet of Jesus, Martha hurried around the kitchen preparing the meal—no small task in those days. Look at the cost Martha was willing to pay to be a good hostess! She was going to sacrifice a private audience with God Incarnate for hours to prepare a single meal.

Do things in your house have to be perfect before you can invite even a few friends over for an evening of fellowship? Paying the price of a perfect house might take away from something more important. Perhaps that's why one of the qualifications for elders is that they must be hospitable. No one can be hospitable without having first wrestled with the Martha problem and decided that people are more important than prepping for a perfect evening.

4. *The time dollars test.* In Thoreau's *Walden* he mentions to a friend that he could walk the distance to a nearby town in less time than he could earn the ninety cents for a train fare to the destination. How many of us have made that type of calculation on our everyday purchases?

Begin thinking of everything you want in terms of the amount of time it will take, after taxes and other deductions, to have enough money to buy that item. Then ask yourself, *What else could I have done with that amount of time? Which is the better use of my time?* Once you start to calculate what things cost in terms of time and freedom, you'll be on your way to changing bad spending habits, says Clint Willis. In his research, Willis found one person who used this method for a month and told him, "We were literally spending $1,000 a year on espresso."

Amy Dacyczyn suggests that you think about what you would do with the time it takes to make the money you spend. How long does it take you to earn $1,000? If something costs $25 per week, it costs $1,090 per year. Throw in childcare and taxes and the cost goes higher. How many $25-a-week habits can you afford? How many can you live without? Sooner or later our possessions begin to possess us with their demands of upkeep, warranties, payments, additional storage space and time to use and enjoy them.

Thinking of possessions in terms of the amount of the finite time it takes to earn them puts a different perspective on our spending. The challenge is to begin to spend less and spend wisely. "When you have a goal, spending less is fun. You can watch yourself reclaim your personal freedom," says Vicki Robin. She suggests the following to help control spending:

1. When an item strikes your fancy, wait a month before buying it to avoid impulse buying.

2. Calculate the true cost of purchases, including taxes and maintenance.

3. Research major purchases by calling several potential sellers.

4. Don't read catalogs; they make buying too effortless.

To the list above we would add an implied, but not enumerated, axiom: *Don't charge what you can't afford.* In "High Interest? It's in the Cards," Danny Boyd reported that

☐ more than half of all consumers carry debt forward on their cards each month

☐ the average American family owes eleven creditors

☐ the average family carries 4.2 bankcards in addition to other cards for gas, department stores and so on

☐ the average family has a bankcard debt of more than $4,000

☐ if only the minimum balance is paid on this $4,000, it will take just under 30 years to repay and will cost more than $10,000 in interest

No matter what method you use to simplify, this point is important: do it big, do it small, but do it now for the sake of your mental, physical and, most important, spiritual health.

Questions for Thought or Discussion

1. When you apply any of the tests to your current priorities or possessions, which stand out as ones you would keep and why? Which would you eliminate and why?

2. Can you think of an example of a possession that began to possess you?

3. Make a list of your $25-a-week habits. How would your life be different if you could turn that $1,000 a year into more time for family, leisure and devotion?

4. In what ways can you "invest in eternity"?

8

....

Six Steps to a Simpler Life

Mike sat at his desk with his head in his hands, massaging his temples.

I wondered how I was going to pull this off. It had been approximately fifteen months since we had purchased our new home. I had just paid a few bills, and already the checkbook balance was zero with the whole month ahead of us. It was a situation that had become all too common over the past several months. We had established and used our lines of credit, and now the debt was mounting.

At first the solution appeared simple to me: work harder, work longer and make more money to afford the lifestyle we were living. It didn't take too many months for me to realize this plan was not going to work.

With my head in my hands, I knew something had to change and soon. Life was actually getting worse, not better. Not only was I around my family less, but I was also finding myself more irritable and fatigued.

Steps to a Simpler Life

By now you may be thinking that right-sizing would be a great idea in theory but might not be practical for you. What follows are the six steps to a simpler life, a process that Mike learned in his efforts to resize his life.

First, share with your spouse (or in the case of singles, another person you trust) your desire and your burden regarding why you want to right-size. Perhaps your reasons are financial, and you are convicted that you are spending too much on things and not enough on God's ministry. Perhaps you're working too hard to keep up with the expenses of your lifestyle. Maybe you're suffering burnout from the need to earn the money it takes to live as you do. Perhaps you're undergoing pain and stress, which has led you to some unhealthy habits such as alcohol abuse or involvement in unhealthy relationships in an attempt to find the energy and renewed desire to work.

Second, agree on the amount of right-sizing that needs to be done. Having been raised on a farm with a very meager income from my parents' jobs, I (Mike) think I could be happy with a small, simple home without a lot of extras. However, I have to admit that I enjoy having friends over and am proud that our home is large enough for guests and decorated nicely enough that people compliment our taste.

But our house is not nearly as important to me as it is to my wife. For this reason we discussed the house situation at length. We settled on a house smaller than the one where we were living and decided on a house payment that our budget could handle. I had to concede some, and she conceded a few things as well. We have now been in this home for more than a year, and already we both feel much relief and are more than content. We wish we had done this several years ago.

Perhaps the right-sizing you need to do does not involve a home at all. Maybe it involves cutting back the amount of time you are spending doing things that do not involve family, such as golfing or hunting. In this regard, it may be less necessary to make financial sacrifices but more necessary to make a sacrifice of your time—right-sizing your lifestyle more than your budget. Again, share this with your spouse, develop a plan and set limits.

Third, pray. After you have laid out your plan with your spouse or a trusted friend, pray that God will give you wisdom, strength and courage to go through with your plans. There are emotional aspects of right-sizing. When I sold the large house and moved into a moderate-sized one, people wondered what my financial problems were. Others had questions that were a bit awkward to answer. Although I was not required to answer, my typical response was that we simply didn't enjoy the house as much as we thought we would and that it was not worth the cost it was extracting from the family. My wife and I prayed about this, and we continued to pray that God would help us to get done what needed to be done.

Fourth, inform the people most affected by your plan. If it involves children, bring them along with your decision. I don't believe that children need to know all the whys, but they do need to know that changes are going to happen and the basic reasons you are right-sizing.

During our right-sizing process my daughter told me a story that showed just how much of a family decision this was. Several months after we shared our decision to right-size with our children, my daughter, during the prayer request time at her Christian school, had her Bible class praying that our home would sell and that our resizing would go smoothly so that our family could be less stressed and that her dad could relax and not have to work as hard at his job.

Fifth, find someone to support you and hold you accountable. Share your plans with a godly person who understands your needs and desires, someone who loves you and will keep your confidence and who feels the same burden you do. The thought that someone is praying for you and even holding you accountable will be a great comfort in the process of right-sizing.

Finally, maintain a positive attitude and smile. Several years ago, I was asked to give a positive, upbeat sermon to kick off a week at youth camp. I developed a sermon that was primarily built around smiling. Living the sermon that week required me to hold my tongue and make positive comments while avoiding negative comments. Incorporate that attitude into your right-sizing effort as you look forward to what it will mean to you.

I have found the changes from right-sizing very rewarding. I still work more than forty hours a week; with on-call weekends and evenings I end up working about fifty hours a week. But my life is much less stressed and hectic. I have fewer headaches. I am able to be home earlier in the day and to take off that occasional afternoon without feeling guilty, since I am no longer pushed by the demand of the bills coming in.

Putting It into Practice

One young woman I saw in my medical practice for about four years had attended a Christian university and then completed her studies in law. She was working as an attorney for the state. After numerous visits with her, primarily for complaints regarding headaches, we had a frank discussion regarding the stress she was living with. She was married to a man who was successful in his field of business, and they had recently had their first child. But when she asked me why she was having so many headaches, I had to be honest. Working in excess of forty hours a week in a pressure-packed job as an attorney, being a wife and being a mother to her newborn daughter were simply more than she could physically and emotionally handle.

But she kept asking, "How do you expect me to pay the bills and continue my career and accomplish the goals I want to accomplish professionally and still do what you say I need to be doing?" We spent some time discussing this and even prayed about it. When she returned the next week, she confessed that she had gone home quite angry and upset about what we had discussed. However, after talking it over with her husband, she had realized that indeed some lifestyle changes were in order.

In the ensuing weeks the couple decided to sell their house

and move into a smaller one, and she decided to work part time. Even though she still has headaches, they are much less frequent and much easier to control.

Needless to say, it was not an easy decision for them to make. It came with some pain and effort, but they believe that their decision was the right one. Yet one reaction did come as a surprise. The woman's father was a bit disappointed that she had made the decision to sell the larger home and right-size. It was as if he saw this as an act of weakness or a failure, rather than as a positive move.

Maybe you're thinking about giving the simpler life a try. Remember that you cannot rush into a life of simplicity without thought and prayer. It is like the parable of the sower, when the seed sprang up rapidly only to be choked out by the weeds. The same thing can happen to those who rush to align their lives more in line with God's will—the cares of the world can spring up and choke even the best of intentions.

The Role of Planning in the Right-Sizing Process

Anyone planning to right-size his or her life must look on the planning process as an important step if the endeavor is to be a success. In an article titled "In Search of a Simpler Life" author Barbara Ehrenreich says that "downshifting, unlike old-fashioned dropping out, often involves as much deliberation and planning as any conventional career move."

Clint Willis knows this is true. He went from a New York publishing career to a freelance writing career. Willis told Ehrenreich that he and his wife made "one big mistake: We relied too heavily on good intentions to control our future spending. After all those years of hailing taxis and going to fancy restaurants, we discovered that we really didn't know how to cut back."

"Before you jump into a new life that might involve a pay cut, do a dry run and trim your living expenses," suggests Peg Downey, a financial planner. "That will help prepare you for the change—and it will also give you a sign that you can really succeed before you burn all your bridges."

Here is a checklist of practical suggestions to follow when attempting to simplify your life. They come from Philip's own attempt to resize his life and his conversations with Christian friends who have similar aspirations.

1. Pray for success in the endeavor before you start and daily thereafter.

2. Start with an attainable goal—perhaps cutting back work hours and spending by 10-15 percent.

3. Cut up and consolidate credit cards.

4. Do a "spring cleaning" on your schedule, looking for time-consuming items that can be eliminated.

5. Don't say yes to anything else without saying no to something you're doing. If not, you'll be forced to steal the time for the new commitment from your family or your sleep.

6. Work to live; don't live to work.

7. Don't fall into the overachiever's trap, thinking that you must excel in every area of life. Average is fine in many areas.

8. Don't make choices today that take away options tomor-

row. Going in debt now means fewer choices about discretion-
ary income in the future.

The Myth of Immediate Reward

Too many Christians have fallen for one of the greatest myths
of our time, which is perpetuated by televangelists and pulpit
ministers alike—the gospel of success. The gospel of success
preaches that the returns God has promised his children when
they give to him will be both immediate and tangible. Yet the
parable of the rich man and Lazarus (Lk 16:19-31), indeed the
whole of Scripture, contradicts this claim and demonstrates
that some inequities will be worked out only in the eternal
realm. What do you think Lazarus would say to a modern
evangelist of the gospel of success who claims that material
blessings are sprinkled on those who please God with their
(tax deductible) gifts?

Jesus promised that God knows our needs and will supply
them. In Matthew 7:9-11 he says,

Which of you, if his son asks for bread, will give him a
stone? Or if he asks for a fish, will give him a snake? If you,
then, though you are evil, know how to give good gifts to
your children, how much more will your Father in heaven
give good gifts to those who ask him!

We are not guaranteed that God will reward us monetarily for
our gifts to him. We may be rewarded in ways that we never
imagined. Perhaps when we give God our money he in turn
gives us continued good health. Perhaps when we give him
our time he gives us strength to live another day. Perhaps when

we give him our energy he rewards us with peaceful sleep.

Parents may find that they attempt to substitute tangible things for the intangible gifts that their children ask of them. Numerous surveys have shown that the most important thing children want from their fathers is more time. Surveys also show that the primary reason fathers give for working long hours is to give good things to their children. Will our children one day say,

☐ "We asked for attention, and you gave us more money"?

☐ "We asked to be made more important in your life, and you bought us more things to occupy our time"?

☐ "We asked you to listen, and you said you'd get back to us"? It seems as though our children are asking for bread and we are giving them stones.

The word *integrity* comes from the Latin *integer,* meaning whole. For instance, a fraction of a number cannot be an integer; only a whole number can. A man or woman of integrity doesn't ignore family or church or the community for the sake of a job. He or she leads a whole life, even if the result is counter to the gospel of success that urges us to rise to the top no matter what the cost.

The Reality of Eventual Reward

In Matthew 19:29 Jesus speaks of the types of sacrifices that resizing one's life involve: "Everyone who has left house or brothers or sisters or father or mother or children or fields for my sake will receive a hundred times as much and will inherit eternal life."

Jesus expected some people to value a relationship with him above even their relationship with their own family. He expected that some of his followers would walk away from their dwelling places and their sources of income to follow him. It's easy to believe that it was simpler for the listeners in Jesus' day to walk away from their homes than it would be for us today. Yet we know from the parables that the people to whom Jesus spoke had landlords and debt, bought property and made payments just like we do. He wasn't speaking to a nomadic culture when he made this perplexing offer. These people were expected to walk away from relative security to a total trust in Jesus.

The model for this behavior is found in the disciples themselves. Several of them left their boats and family business to follow Jesus. Matthew gave up what amounted to a tax franchise to join the Twelve. At one point in Jesus' ministry, when the crowds had started to turn away from his hard teachings, Jesus asked his disciples if they also would be leaving him. Peter voiced the opinion of the group when he said, "Lord, to whom shall we go? You have the words of eternal life" (Jn 6:68).

According to Matthew 19:29, the benefits of following Jesus apparently come both in this life and in the life to come. Note the payoff: a hundred times as much *and* eternal life. God will reward the leap of faith both now and in the future. But there is no assurance that the payoff will come in monetary form. It might come in a less tangible form such as contentment, freedom from guilt, peace of mind, better relationships with

our friends, or God-fearing children. If that isn't a one-hun-
dredfold return, what is?

Questions for Thought or Discussion

1. Is there someone you trust enough to hold you accountable
for any lifestyle decisions you make after prayerful consideration?

2. Do you know a person of integrity? How does he or she
demonstrate the qualities of wholeness that the word implies?

3. What is the best gift you have ever given your children? Why
do you think that it was good?

9

....

Redefining
Success

*Mike recently had a humbling experience that taught him a lesson
in servanthood.*

I had made the decision to open my practice to a health
maintenance organization (HMO). After experiencing several frustrations with the HMO, I called for a meeting with
the physician who was the program administrator.

In the course of the conversation, I complained about
having no control over the patients who selected me as their
primary physician and even singled out one patient whom
I referred to as "difficult." The answer of the administrator
surprised me.

"Doctor," she said, "we can take this patient off your list
if you desire, but whose responsibility is it to take care of
the difficult patients?"

I had to admit that I had lost sight of the reason I decided to be a physician twenty years ago. Was I called to be a financially successful doctor in my community, or was I called to give medical help to people who need it regardless of their social status, health problems or personality?

Philip had a similar experience in his role as chair of a university department.

I remember holding a faculty meeting, spending a great deal of time talking about a few problem students and expressing a desire for the time when we could just "graduate them and not take in any more like them." Then a faculty member reminded me: "Perhaps they're the ones we have been called to serve."

It dawned on me that the well-prepared and socially skilled students hardly need my counsel. My main job for them is not to hinder their progress through college on the way to a successful career. Yet my true job is to help the less prepared and the social misfits to find their place in the professional community upon graduation.

A Call for Servants

Servants are needed everywhere: in the home, in the classroom, in the church, on the Little League field. Servants lead by taking the lowliest position and doing it so well and so cheerfully that others begin to notice. In making this paradigm shift from leader-as-boss to leader-as-servant, we are obeying the command to follow Jesus' example found in Philippians 2:5-8.

Your attitude should be the same as that of Christ Jesus:

Who, being in very nature God,

did not consider equality with God something to be
   grasped,
but made himself nothing,
   taking the very nature of a servant,
   being made in human likeness.
And being found in appearance as a man,
   he humbled himself
   and became obedient to death—
      even death on a cross!

In calling his followers to lead a life of sacrifice, Jesus led the
way by making the greatest sacrifice of all—giving up his life.

Why is Christ qualified to lead the church? Because he laid
down his life for it. What should we as parents lay down to
lead in our homes? Should we lay down our pens? Our law
books? Our stethoscopes? Put away our computers? If we're
truly willing to lay down our lives for our families, shouldn't
we be willing to lay down our work after we have earned
enough to provide the basic necessities of life?

Changing Our Viewpoint

One way to get out of the busyness-equals-success trap is to
change the paradigm from which we view success. Jesus said,
"If anyone wants to be first, he must be the very last, and the
servant of all" (Mk 9:35). Yet how many Christians do you see
scrambling for the bottom rungs of the ladder of success?

John Robinson, coauthor of *Time for Life,* suggests that we
like to say we are busy because being busy makes us powerful.
People who arrive at a meeting late are seen as more powerful

than those who arrive early. Similarly, those who have enough time to pursue a leisurely hobby seem inferior to those who take their cellular phone to the golf course and zip through a round in three hours. "As you say time is more important to you, you become more important yourself," Robinson concludes.

Perhaps that's why author Barbara Ehrenreich calls downshifting "a serious psychic undertaking."

Success, for most of us, has meant being in the loop, having more phone messages and faxes than we can answer, scurrying into meetings ten minutes late. Measuring success in a new way—as calm and deliberate achievement instead of frenetic busyness—takes some getting used to. Work after all is much more than a means to an end. In standard American usage, "hardworking" is synonymous with "decent," "reliable" and possibly "saved." Professionals especially tend to confuse work with self, and even to see mere busyness as a mark of status.

When we change our paradigm of what constitutes a well-lived day, perhaps we'll see that leading by serving is the way to achieve the balanced life.

Christ the Servant

In the fall of 1995 I (Mike) was caught up in being a doctor while losing my grip at home, at church and even in the medical practice I was working on so hard. I was as burned out as I had ever been when I was asked to teach a university students' Bible class on the Gospel of John. When I got to the story of the upper room, it dawned on me that this wasn't merely a story about humility—this was a lesson in servanthood.

On the eve of his betrayal, Jesus gathered the Twelve together for their final meal together and led not by words but by example. He stood up from the table, took off his outer clothes, picked up a towel and began to do the unthinkable— washed his disciples' feet, the lowliest job imaginable.

Why did Jesus wash his disciples' feet? To make for a more pleasant last meal? No. Jesus washed those feet because he knew he was about to go away and he had one more lesson that he wished to reinforce. While the Holy Spirit would soon follow Jesus and make the disciples bold, they needed an image to show them how to be servants. They had been instructed in matters Jesus considered critical, and now they would be shown how to serve. They had to think less of themselves and more of others. And Jesus provided a perfect illustration.

Later he told them: "A new command I give you: Love one another. As I have loved you, so you must love one another" (Jn 13:34). On the surface this doesn't look like a new command, but what is new is not that they are to love one another but the quality of love that they are to have. He was telling them to care about their brother's clean feet more than their own hungry stomach, to think of others first and self last. And in a few hours he would illustrate this principle dramatically by dying for them.

In studying Christ's model I felt the call to quit worrying about having a good month financially and to begin being a servant to the patients who had entrusted their health to my care. Suddenly the mental cobwebs entangling my medical practice were swept aside, and I had a clear focus of why I became a physician in the first place.

Testing God's Will

Paul instructs us in Romans 12:1-2,

> Therefore, I urge you, brothers, in view of God's mercy, to offer your bodies as living sacrifices, holy and pleasing to God—this is your spiritual act of worship. Do not conform any longer to the pattern of this world, but be transformed by the renewing of your mind. Then you will be able to test and approve what God's will is—his good, pleasing and perfect will.

The last part of the passage is the most often overlooked. Until we climb on the altar of sacrifice and become as servants, we'll never know what God's will is for our lives. What a sobering thought: God's will to work through us and our chosen profession to his glory may go undiscovered because we haven't placed ourselves in the right posture to get the lesson.

In *The Seven Habits of Highly Effective Families,* Stephen Covey makes the point that an airplane traveling between two distant airports is rarely directly on track to the final destination. Instead the entire trip involves constant, minor adjustments by the pilot and the instruments to navigate the plane to its final destination.

The same is true with families. Those that have an ultimate final destination—heaven—will find a way to stay on track. And while daily or seasonal adjustments might have to be made, having a keen sense of the final destination will aid us in the journey.

God's promise of direction comes to those who have learned to submit to him. That is both a comforting and a frightening thought. It is comforting that he will lead us where he wants us. It is frightening that he will not reveal his will for us until we climb up on that altar with both body and mind and say, "God, I hope this sacrifice pleases you."

Stepping off the Fast Track

A great symphony conductor was once asked what was the most difficult instrument to play. He replied, "Second fiddle—because nobody wants to play it." A wonderful illustration of someone willing to play the hardest of all instruments comes from 1954, when two men played second fiddle to Roger Bannister and in doing so helped him change forever both the world of track and field and our ideas of human boundaries.

In 1954 the four-minute mile stood as a barrier that many experts felt would never be broken. The world record was 4:01.4 and had been set in 1945, and the holder of that mark was retired. Articles were written about the physical impossibility of the task. It seemed as absurd as putting a man on the moon and about as distant.

Even if the mark was to be broken, no one was watching an obscure Oxford medical student named Roger Bannister, whose personal best in the race was 4:03.6. Bannister knew from his medical studies that the claims that people were not physiologically capable of going under the four-minute mile were nonsense. And he also had a novel strategy to break the barrier. So he set his eyes on the goal of a world record and the magic time. He chose a two-way meet between Oxford and the Amateur Athletic Association on May 6, 1954, to try it.

His plan was to get two elite runners to help him with the pace necessary to break the mark. His helpers would set the right pace, and Bannister would follow. At designated points in the race his pacers would step off the track, leaving Bannister to finish. Chris Brasher was to help for the first half, and Chris Chataway was to help for the third quarter, leaving Bannister alone and on pace for the final quarter-mile lap.

The race day came, and Bannister lined up with his teammates and opponents. Brasher led for the first half-mile, stepping off the track at the midway point after having set a pace of 1:58. Chataway took it from there, leading for a quarter mile and stepping off the track, having kept a pace of 3:00.7 for the first three-quarters of a mile. It was now up to Bannister.

Paced by his friends and now summoning all his energy, Bannister ran the last lap in less than 59 seconds. His world record of 3:59.4 won the race and created one of the greatest stirs the athletic world was to see in the decade of the 1950s. In his victory lap, Bannister called his two friends back to the track, and together they celebrated the new record.

Why would two elite, world-class athletes take themselves out of a race by serving as pacesetters? They believed in the goal, and the goal required that two runners be servants in the process. They performed their roles in achieving the goal and stepped off the track.

In the same way, why would a parent step off the career track of promotions and advancement to give more attention to the family? Why would a parent step off the track of a full-time job in favor of a part-time one to be at home to rear the children? Why would a single adult decide to work less in exchange for having more time to do the Lord's work? Because such people believe in the goal of going to heaven and taking those that they love with them, and the goal requires the heart of a servant.

Leading through servanthood will change the way we spend our time and arrange our priorities like never before. We will no longer be able to routinely come home too late and too exhausted to be a spouse and a parent. We will no longer routinely interrupt or miss family time for some good work we volunteered to do. We will no longer believe the myth that quality time will be sufficient for our families.

Changing the paradigm of leadership in our homes and our careers will be painful at first, but the payoffs are worth the pain. Once we decide to lead through a life of service, relationships will heal, stress-related physical problems will diminish and our spiritual lives will be strengthened.

Questions for Thought or Discussion

1. How does one acquire the attitude of Jesus that Paul refers to in the passage on servanthood in Philippians 2?

2. What should you lay down in your life in order to serve your family better?

3. When you feel burned out, what is usually the cause? What is the solution?

10

Taking the Leap of Faith
Will God Catch Us?

A few years ago a young woman in our congregation was suffering from brain cancer, which eventually claimed her life. One Sunday after her initial weeks of treatment, she was able to return to worship. Mike's daughter, Addi, seven years old at the time, saw her entering the auditorium. She sprang up and went to meet her in the aisle.

"Are you well yet?" she asked.

"Not quite yet, sweetheart," was the reply.

"Well, how long will it take?" Addi asked.

In her simple, childlike faith, Addi had prayed, God had heard her, and she just didn't understand why the illness wasn't already taken care of. As adults, our challenge is to recapture that innocent faith that trusts an all-powerful God to deliver when we pray.

Two Types of Faith

While we sometimes think of faith as a singular quality, in reality Christians are asked to have two different kinds of faith. The first type is no problem for most Christians, but it is a major stumbling block for the rest of the world—a fact predicted by Paul in 1 Corinthians 1. This faith asks us to believe that God came to earth in the form of a baby, the son of an unremarkable carpenter and his virgin wife-to-be in an obscure village. Furthermore, we are called to believe that this baby would be the Lamb of God crucified for our sins.

Many people refuse to take up this faith. Either they don't believe in their lost condition or the power of God to save, or they simply don't care. These people have to make the present eternal in their lives because they refuse to make the eternal present.

The second kind of faith is that which acknowledges that God will take care of the physical needs of his children just as he took care of their spiritual needs. Paul writes that each Christian should "work out your salvation with fear and trembling" (Phil 2:12). Paul wasn't referring to negotiating with God for the forgiveness of sins. What must be worked out with God is his offer of sustenance and how we respond to it. How much of our God-given time will we spend acquiring what he has already promised will be there? It's an important question because it determines how much time will be left for God and for our families.

Needless to say, a faith this simple is problematic for many. Can we take the promises of Matthew 6:25-34 literally? Will God clothe us, feed us, shelter us as he does the birds of the air and the rest of nature? If so, what is the role of our labor in this process? The psalmist writes,

Unless the LORD builds the house,
   its builders labor in vain.
Unless the LORD watches over the city,
   the watchmen stand guard in vain.
In vain you rise early
   and stay up late,
toiling for food to eat—
   for he grants sleep to those he loves. (Ps 127:1-2)

If the outcome of labor is preordained by God, what we are left to wrestle with is how much we do on our own and how much we leave to faith.

The problem comes when our inability to grasp this second kind of faith—that God will supply our daily needs—kicks us into a cycle of overwork that depletes our time for spiritual contemplation. Jesus said, "Be careful, or your hearts will be weighed down with dissipation, drunkenness and the anxieties of life, and that day will close on you unexpectedly like a trap" (Lk 21:34). We can get so weighed down with the anxieties of life that the coming of the Lord takes us by surprise.

The parable of the ten bridesmaids in Matthew 25 describes such a surprise visit to those who were unprepared. Why did five of the women not have oil for their lamps? Did they think the bridegroom was not coming? An engagement in Jesus' day was about as binding as marriage itself, so the bridegroom was surely coming. Why then was half of the wedding party not ready for his appearance? Could it be that in the busyness of the day they forgot about the business of preparing for his coming? And we can ask this question of ourselves: In anticipation of Jesus' sure return, have we left anything undone in our busy lives?

Why Worry?

When Mary sat at the feet of Jesus as her sister Martha scrambled to prepare a meal, Jesus told Martha, "You are worried and upset about many things, but only one thing is needed. Mary has chosen what is better" (Lk 10:41-42). Mary worried about the lasting words of salvation; Martha worried about the food. Notice that the two worries were mutually exclusive—you can't worry about spiritual and physical food at the same time.

Jesus addressed the problems of worry in Matthew 6:25. What can worry *not* do? The list is long. It can't add an hour to your life, feed you, clothe you or shelter you. But worrying about all these things can distract you from being ready for Christ when he comes or when you are called to go to him.

So what's the solution? It comes in three steps: Say no, give thanks and look up.

Say no. Titus 2:11-13 tells us:

The grace of God that brings salvation has appeared to all men. It teaches us to say "No" to ungodliness and worldly passions, and to live self-controlled, upright and godly lives in this present age, while we wait for the blessed hope—the glorious appearing of our great God and Savior, Jesus Christ.

We are first assured that salvation is attainable, and then we are commanded to say no to the worldly passions that would encumber us from accepting it. Is a larger house a worldly passion? A better car? A promotion? A second job? Each individual must decide, and each individual must be willing to say no when these passions tempt.

Give thanks. Ecclesiastes 5:19 and Ecclesiastes 6:2 are very similar. In the first God gives a man "wealth and possessions, and enables him to enjoy them." The result is happiness. In the second "God gives a man wealth, possessions and honor, so that he lacks nothing his heart desires, but God does not enable him to enjoy them, and a stranger enjoys them instead. This is meaningless, a grievous evil."

The point is that for some people there is never enough. Remember the illustration of labor leader Samuel Gompers, who said that the American worker simply wanted "more"? While a decent wage is certainly important, there's never an end to "more." "More" is a standard that rises with each new acquisition. And to those who lack the ability to enjoy what God has blessed them with, no accomplishment, no raise, no amount of possessions will ever be enough.

The two men in Ecclesiastes 5 and 6 were both blessed. The difference is that one knew it and the other didn't. We must realize that we Americans are blessed far above 95 percent of the world. But do we act like it? Do we thank God for it? Do we stop our labors long enough to enjoy it? We all know people who have given up a hobby such as golf or quilting because they "just don't have time anymore." What is the fruit of our labor for if not to relax occasionally and reflect on how good God has been to us?

Look up. We should follow the admonition of Paul to the Colossians when he tells them, "Set your minds on things above, not on earthly things. For you died, and your life is now hidden with Christ in God" (Col 3:2-3). Christians shouldn't look around; we should look up. Looking around begins the endless cycle of desiring name-brand clothing, better cars, fancier landscaping and all the rest. Looking up breaks the cycle. Christians should compare themselves to only one standard: Jesus, who said, "For where your treasure is, there your heart will be also" (Mt 6:21). He is looking to see where our hearts lie by seeing where we're casting our eyes.

The Risk of Possessions

Did Jesus say this to call us to lives of poverty? Hardly. Jesus said this to keep us from a life of slavery to our possessions. He knew that the time for spiritual things is choked out by the accumulation of physical things. For instance, owning a boat demands time at and on the lake. Once the purchase is made, the time must follow. And if the only time available to go to the lake is on Sunday, worship takes a back seat to the possession, which now possesses us, demanding several weekends a year of our time.

Does that make certain possessions like a boat inherently bad? Certainly not. But it does make it inherently risky. With every additional possession, we run the risk that those possessions and their upkeep will drive a wedge between us and God. "Seek first his kingdom and his righteousness, and all these things will be given to you as well" (Mt 6:33). It's a command, not a cosmic gamble. And in the context of the Sermon on the Mount, it's a radical new idea.

Even in an era that was primitive by our standards, Christ's listeners were not living a simple life. There were taxes to pay, landlords to satisfy. Yet he did not say, "Keep seeking the kingdom first and I will take care of you." He said, in effect, "Start seeking the kingdom first and I will take care of you." He was calling them to a change in lifestyle: to seek the kingdom first and put their trust in God for all the rest.

In Luke 18:8 Jesus asks, "When the Son of Man comes, will he find faith on the earth?" Notice that he didn't ask if he would find any religious activity or any good works being done. He assumed that would be the case.

Jesus will undoubtedly return to find a pragmatic faith, a faith that believes intellectually in the power of the crucified and resurrected Jesus to save us from our sins. But the gut-level faith that says God will put a safety net under us if we walk out on that wire with him might be hard to find. It's as if our faith can stretch only so far. We'll accept the supernatural—the virgin birth, the empty tomb—but don't ask us to accept the tangible. "Will he not much more clothe you, O you of little faith?" (Mt 6:30).

Taking the Leap

In a scene from the movie *Indiana Jones and the Last Crusade*, the archaeologist hero is attempting to find the Holy Grail—a cup used by Christ himself. But to get there he has to face a series of obstacles, including the "leap of faith," where he takes a step off a cliff, hoping and trusting that an invisible bridge will appear.

We're called on to make a similar leap each day. Each of us is required to make leaps of faith that if we put God first, he will step in and provide for our needs. Should we still work at our jobs? Yes. That's been a part of God's plan since Adam and Eve left the Garden of Eden. But, to paraphrase the psalmist, our times will be in his hands—our starting times, our quitting times, our family times (see Ps 31:15). We will trust him that a reasonable amount of work will yield an adequate amount of income for our families.

The Christian walk becomes a two-step process—releasing our grip on our lives and grasping the hand of God. Letting go of our grip on our lives can sometimes be the easy part—repenting of our sins and turning away from our previous lives that were leading us to death. Grasping the hand of God and letting him lead is the hard part. It means turning away from self-reliance to God-reliance—stepping out in faith when the bridge can't been seen yet. This second part is that which many never understand, resulting in lives being tugged in two directions.

Tugged in Two Directions

In *The Simple Life* Vernard Eller calls the idea of a simple Christian life a dialectical teaching—one that pulls us two ways at once. Eller compares it to a Ping-Pong ball placed in the airstream coming out of a vacuum that is blowing air out. It is first pushed by the air, then pulled by gravity, then pushed, then pulled. The result is that the ball seemingly dances in space, held there by the laws of physics.

So it is with the Christian caught between the mandate of the simple life found in Christ's teachings in the Sermon on the Mount and the very real tug of the world. Think of Matthew 6 as the push that gets you to soar and the realities of bills and work as the force of gravity bringing you down.

Some Christians do quite well at balancing the complexity of daily living with biblical commands and hover between them like the Ping-Pong ball. Others stay permanently grounded. Consider the apostle Peter when he attempted to walk on the water. After Peter asked Jesus if he could come to him on the water, Peter actually did it. But then he saw the waves and began to sink. When he took his eyes off Jesus and began to think of the impossibility of what he was doing, his faith lapsed, and so did his footing.

The same is true with us. Christian simplicity is a lifestyle as tenuous as walking on the water. What about health care? What about the best colleges for my children? What about retirement? All these questions must be answered. But worrying about them becomes the waves that will sink us. Even while we ask these important questions, we must never take our eyes off Jesus. Only Jesus can help us walk on the troubled waters of modern life.

Changing the Way We Act *and* Think
Grasping this second kind of faith—reliance on God for our daily needs—is a physical and a mental process. Paul offers this challenge in Romans 12:2: "Do not conform any longer to the pattern of this world, but be transformed by the renewing of your mind." The mental process must go along with the

physical. We have to change the way we think at the same time we change the way we act.

Suppose you are trying to lose weight. One way would be to change the way you "act" at the table—eating smaller portions and less fatty foods. Another way would be to change the way you act by exercising more. But the truly successful dieters will also change the way they think. They will change the way they look at food. They will eat to live, not live to eat. They will look at diet as only one component of a lifestyle that includes exercise and will make the proper adjustments. These will be the successful dieters—those who change both the way they act and the way they think.

The same is true with successful downshifters. They will change their actions and their outlook at the same time. They will work to live, not live to work. They will spend both quality time and quantity time with their children.

In the Old Testament story of Gideon in Judges 6—8, God ordered Gideon to downsize the army that would be going up against the Midianites. Eventually Gideon sent nearly thirty-two thousand men home, leaving him only three hundred to fight the mighty Midianite army. God's reason is recounted in Judges 7:2 when he tells Gideon that he was cutting back the army so that no one in Israel could "boast . . . that her own strength has saved her."

The angel of the Lord calls Gideon a "mighty warrior" at their first encounter, even though Gideon was hiding in a winepress threshing grain and hoping that the Midianites wouldn't discover him. Nothing in his humble background would indicate that he would be the leader of his people. But God has often picked ordinary people to do extraordinary things. Notice then that once God calls you, he empowers you. With only three hundred men left to fight, Gideon had to know that it was God who supplied the victory.

God has called each of us to fight for him, not against pagan armies, but against the "powers of this dark world and against the spiritual forces of evil in the heavenly realms" (Eph 6:12). Those fighting God's battles today may not look like mighty warriors, but they can be if they have the faith of Gideon that God will supply the victory. And God will get the credit for the extraordinary lives we lead in these ordinary bodies.

God will not give us everything we ask for in prayer. He will not heal every disease or restore every broken relationship. He will not even prevent bankruptcy or divorce from striking some of his children. The reason God will not supply a miracle to heal every illness of his children is that the true miracle does not occur when a cancer goes into remission. The true miracle occurs when the child of God gets cancer and refuses to lose his or her faith in the process.

Because of this, God will never make his people uniformly wealthy or successful or healthy. If we live upright lives of godliness and sacrifice, it is not because God fulfills our every desire if we follow him. Instead we follow God because we trust that if we do, he will supply our needs—not all our wants, but our needs.

Just as God knew precisely how many men Gideon needed to accomplish his purpose, he knows precisely the measure of health and wealth we need to accomplish our purpose here on earth. Our job is to trust him to supply what we need to defeat the enemy.

Questions for Thought or Discussion

1. What are the roadblocks to accepting the first type of faith? The second type of faith?

2. If a person possesses faith in God to save but lacks faith in God to provide, what types of behaviors will he or she exhibit?

3. How do we reconcile the promises of Matthew 6 with the practical necessity that we must provide for our families?

4. Are there any things in your life that you need to say no to?

5. What are some possessions that might be inherently "risky" for Christians due to the lifestyle change they will require or the physical toll it will take to pay for them?

11

....

Passing It On
to the Next
Generation

The city in which I (Mike) practice medicine seems to have an epidemic of overspending. The stress this brings with it has far-reaching consequences. By some estimates Americans spend 1.4 dollars for every dollar they earn, so it's no wonder that headaches, fatigue, insomnia and stomach pain are among the most common presenting complaints in my office.

I see people every day who are struggling with depression, anxiety, and emotional and physical burnout. Many of them have never been taught how to live life, something that is critically important yet has often been overlooked by busy parents. This chapter presents five basic principles that a person must adhere to in order to avoid some of life's problems.

While we sometimes battle influenza in the winter months, we more often battle what a recent PBS special called "affluenza," an "epidemic of stress, overwork, shopping and debt caused by the dogged pursuit of the American Dream." Here are some signs that we as a nation are in the middle of an epidemic of "affluenza."

☐ The United States has only 5 percent of the world's population yet consumes a third of its resources.

☐ In 1996 more Americans declared bankruptcy (1.1 million) than graduated from college.

☐ In 90 percent of divorce cases, arguments about money play a prominent role.

☐ Americans carry one trillion dollars in personal debt—approximately four thousand dollars for every adult and child, not including home mortgage debt.

I (Mike) want my son, Adam, to avoid these mistakes. So when we recently went on a backpacking trip in Colorado, I planned ahead to discuss some issues with my son that had long been on my heart. Some of these had to do with the birds and the bees, but more than anything else I wanted to share with him some guidelines for his life. The rest of the chapter is what I discussed with him—the five basic elements to living a nonstressed, productive and fulfilling Christian life.

Fear God and Keep His Commandments

God is to be feared and his commandments are to be kept at all costs. We should not expect our kids to be perfect, and God does not expect them to be perfect either. I believe that the rule by which life should be lived is found in Ecclesiastes

12:13-14. Solomon concluded his book by saying,

Now all has been heard;
here is the conclusion of the matter:
Fear God and keep his commandments,
for this is the whole duty of man.
For God will bring every deed into judgment,
including every hidden thing,
whether it is good or evil.

No matter what life throws at us, whether good or bad, success or failure, wealth or poverty, excellent health or poor health, the essence of our lives should be to fear God and keep his commandments.

We live during a time when fearing God is explained as nothing more than respecting God as a greater being. God's nature has not changed since the beginning of time. God expects us not only to respect him but to know that he will carry out just punishment for the sins we commit. Following God's instruction booklet leads to a more fulfilling and healthy life in the here and now.

Solomon is saying in these verses, "I have had it all and I have seen it all, and if I could do it over again, my aim in life would be to fear God and hold steadfastly to his commands." Can you imagine the man who had riches beyond your wildest imagination and the respect of the entire world saying in the end, "It was all meaningless"?

Christ Died for Us

It is easy to forget to understand and realize exactly what it was that Jesus Christ did for us and how important it was. First Corinthians 15:3-4 is a good corrective.

> For what I have received I passed on to you as of first importance: that Christ died for our sins according to the Scriptures, that he was buried, that he was raised on the third day according to the Scriptures.

Just as Solomon had a recipe for a successful life, Paul also told the Corinthians what was most important for them to do. No matter what else you do in life, remember that without Jesus Christ you would be lost and your successes would be meaningless. We should encourage each other and our children to remember daily that Jesus is our Savior.

God Is Good and He Is Present

When Adam and I went hiking with the backdrop of the beautiful Rocky Mountains, the river flowing next to the hiking trail and the greenery surrounding us, nature itself confirmed that God was good and God was present. The presence of God is something that this world does not encourage us to believe in. The world encourages us to be all that we can be on our own. It does not encourage us to let God help us. But God is around at all times, whether in our bedrooms at night or in the Rocky Mountains.

Author Edwin White claims that children have an instinctive sense of God's presence in their lives. He is not just "out there" to be called on in a time of need; he is there. God is around us and with us right now, and he will always be so. We must never lose the sense of God's presence in our lives.

Second Kings 6 tells the story of the king of Aram, who went to the city of Dothan, where Elisha lived, and surrounded it with his armies. When Elisha's servant went out the next morning and saw the forces massed all around, his words said it all: "Oh, my lord, what shall we do?" Elisha calmly replied, "LORD, open his eyes so he may see. . . . Those who are with us are more than those who are with them" (see 2 Kings 6:15-18). At that point the servant's eyes were opened, and he saw a host of angels surrounding the army of Aram. The servant understood why Elisha was not concerned.

We must remember and tell our children that those who are with us are more than those who are with them. We can call on the Lord when we are surrounded by adversity.

It's What's on the Inside That Counts

The prophet Samuel went to visit the house of Jesse to anoint the second king of Israel. Jesse's sons passed before him one by one. The oldest, Eliab, came first. Samuel saw what a handsome man he was and thought surely this would be the next king. What God said to Samuel is as profound now as it was then: "Man looks at the outward appearance, but the LORD looks at the heart" (1 Sam 16:7).

One Sunday a few years ago, a college student came before our congregation with a request. He asked that the church pray for him so that he could be the person on the inside that he was on the outside. Outwardly he appeared to be a great Christian leader on campus, but on the inside he just wasn't what he wanted to be, and he didn't live up to what others thought he was. That should have been the prayer of everyone in the worship service that morning: "Lord, help me to be on the inside what it appears I am on the outside."

The world is a trap waiting for us to buy in to the false presumption that you are worth something if you dress right, if you live in the right neighborhood and if you drive the right kind of car. Once you make those decisions, you're trapped in an endless cycle of work, spend and work some more to pay off the charges. But we must never forget that God does not look at the outward appearance as people do, but instead at the heart.

Every Parent Should Put Family Above Work

I recently took a survey of sixty people in a Bible class, asking them to rank several things in their life in order of importance. They listed God, spouse, children, job, entertainment, worship, physical fitness and others. Without hesitation everyone stated that God was number one in their lives. They explained that if God was the most important thing in our lives, everything else would fall into its proper order. Many felt their spouse should be second; others felt their worship should be second. What was interesting was that jobs were listed fifth or sixth on most people's lists.

After we listed things in their order of importance, I asked the class to list in order from first to last what they spent most of their time doing. Obviously work was number one, as most people in the class spent one-third or more of their lives at work. Interestingly, most spent two or three times more hours watching TV than in worship or in meaningful communication with their spouse. Almost all the members of the class responded that if they weren't so tired, they would have more time to spend with their spouse or their children in meaningful pursuits.

Then I made a confession to the class, approximately a third of whom were my patients. I told them that as patients they simply were not as important to me as my wife and children are.

We have developed a mentality that our jobs are supreme and all else comes in second. This is especially difficult to confront in a profession such as family medicine. But the question remains: When 5:00 p.m. comes and patients are calling and my wife is home with four children, where do my priorities lie? Do I tell the patient who is sick to come on down and I will stay late? Typically it takes forty-five minutes to an hour to catch up on the loose ends of paperwork and dictation at the end of the day. Consequently, I am lucky if I am home by 6:30 p.m., even if I stop seeing patients at 5:30 p.m.

Several years ago I was looking at a picture of my son as a three-year-old. I realized that I didn't remember much about him at that age. I hadn't spent much time with him. I didn't know his habits. I wanted to recall those things so desperately, but the memories just weren't there. I then realized that he was currently eight years old and there were things I was missing out on because I wasn't available most of the time. That's when I decided that my medical patients no longer came first. It took me seven years of medical practice to learn this difficult lesson. I'm thankful that I learned it in time. And I hope that the next generation will learn from my mistakes.

Today, after a regimen of right-sizing my life, I am enjoying my family and my medical practice more than before. I am also enjoying the spiritual benefits that came with restoring my inner peace.

It was only after making these changes in my life that I was able to effectively pass along these five principles to my son. As long as I was living a "meaningless" life, to quote Solomon, my example overwhelmed the words. As I now face up to the task of living these principles, I am in a much stronger position to ask the same of my son as he grows into the man God would have him to be.

Questions for Thought or Discussion

1. Based on the definition of *affluenza* given, have any of its symptoms crept into your life?

2. Has debt ever caused you to stay in a job you didn't like or take a second job you really didn't want to take in order to handle it?

3. In addition to the points above, what other principles do you want to pass on to your children?

12

Go for It

A young girl immigrated to the U.S. from her native Cuba. A devout Catholic, she was faithful in going to confession. Even though she wasn't fluent in English, there was one priest who spoke Spanish. But she knew he wouldn't be there one particular day, so she asked a friend to translate her sins into English and write them on a slip of paper for her to read.

She went into the booth and started by repeating in English the phrase she had heard people around her use: "Forgive me, Father, for I have sinned. It has been a week since my last confession." She then looked down at the list she was to read and discovered that it was too dark in the booth to read. She started, faltered, and then, frustrated, gave up.

"Forgive me, Father," she said. "I can't see my sins."

How many of us can stand outside ourselves and take an objective look at what we've become? Do workaholics know they are suffering? Do obsessive housekeepers know they are obsessive? No. We often can't see our own sins until the ramifications of those sins—an early heart attack, a divorce, problems with children—manifest themselves. *Often changes occur over such a long period of time that we don't even recognize we've changed.*

What has been missing from your life so long that you no longer miss it? Devotional time? A good prayer life? Long talks with your spouse or children?

One place to start understanding our sin is in discerning what is real in our lives. When Philip and Linda took a group of college students to Florence, Italy, they got an object lesson in learning to differentiate the real from the fake.

Our guide warned us that among the scores of leather sellers in the marketplace there would be those selling fake leather. He warned us that the fakes would be so good that we wouldn't be able to tell the difference by feeling or even smelling. The fake leather vendors even had a way of putting lighter fluid on the surface and lighting it in an attempt to show that it wasn't meltable vinyl.

"How can you tell the real thing?" he was asked.

"The only way you can tell the genuine thing is the cost," he replied. "The real leather will always cost more than the fake."

After two days in Florence most of the group had found something leather to take home as a souvenir—belts, purses, briefcases and even jackets. And we all became "leather critics," spotting what we thought were the fakes that we had so smartly avoided.

A few days later, after we had arrived back at our home base of Vienna, I met a young woman from an Islamic nation who had become a Christian during her stay in Austria. I found out that she was no longer welcome in her Islamic home. In the words of Jesus, she had left mother and father, brother and sister for his name. She would be remaining in Vienna and was hoping to get a visa so her stay could be legal and permanent.

It dawned on me that her weeks-old Christianity had already cost her more than my years-old Christianity had cost me. I wondered if the "coat" of Christianity that I wore looked like vinyl to her. I wondered if I could give up everything I had surrounded myself with in my life back in the U.S.—homes, cars and so on—if that's what God required.

Jesus taught that the cost of eternal life would be great. That was the lesson he gave the rich young ruler in Matthew 19. "Teacher," the young man asked, "what good thing must I do to get eternal life?" As he heard the requirements—don't murder, don't commit adultery, don't steal—he must have rejoiced at the possibility of getting eternal life for observing rules that he had already been keeping. "All these I have kept," he said. "What do I still lack?"

Think of how his joy must have faded to disappointment when he heard Jesus say, "If you want to be perfect, go, sell your possessions and give to the poor, and you will have treasure in heaven. Then come, follow me" (Mt 19:16-21). The man was living a good life, but it was a life of illusion, just like the fake leather. And when Jesus offered him real life, he didn't want to pay the cost. The real will always cost more than the fake.

Making Sense of the Commands

Does it make any sense to trust God as completely as we're commanded to in Matthew 6:25-34? Like Abraham when he was asked to sacrifice his only son, we are being asked to make an extremely costly sacrifice—giving up control of our lives and livelihood to God—with only our faith in him as a safety net under us. Look again at the familiar passage in Matthew 6:25-34.

Therefore I tell you, do not worry about your life, what you will eat or drink; or about your body, what you will wear. Is not life more important than food, and the body more important than clothes? Look at the birds of the air; they do not sow or reap or store away in barns, and yet your heavenly Father feeds them. Are you not much more valuable than they? Who of you by worrying can add a single hour to his life?

And why do you worry about clothes? See how the lilies of the field grow. They do not labor or spin. Yet I tell you that not even Solomon in all his splendor was dressed like one of these. If that is how God clothes the grass of the field, which is here today and tomorrow is thrown into the fire, will he not much more clothe you, O you of little faith? So do not worry, saying, "What shall we eat?" or "What shall we drink?" or "What shall we wear?" For the pagans run after all these things, and your heavenly Father knows that you need them. But seek first his kingdom and his righteousness, and all these things will be given to you as well. Therefore do not worry about tomorrow, for tomorrow will worry about itself. Each day has enough trouble of its own.

This passage is not about denying ourselves the necessities of life. God is not asking us to sacrifice all our worldly possessions; he is asking us to give up the driver's seat of our lives. He is asking us to be passengers on a divine journey to the final destination of heaven with a driver who is none other than the creator and clothier of the birds of the air and flowers of the field.

The question we must answer is the same one Abraham had to answer: will we sacrifice our destiny? It won't be the literal sacrifice of a son, but it might mean saying no to a job promotion after prayerful consideration. It might mean changing jobs to one more conducive to family life. It might mean a smaller house so the children can have a Christian education. And what is the reason for making such a counter-cultural decision? The same one Abraham used: God can raise the dead. This life of sacrifice is but a prelude to a life of riches ready for us on the other side.

When Life Gives a Reality Check

Elaine St. James in her book *Inner Simplicity* recounts how her family got an important reality check on what really matters in an unexpected way.

One night, while we were still living in the big house, a huge firestorm came through our area, and we had to evacuate.

Just before we left the house, we looked around and realized how much of the stuff we'd accumulated we could easily get along without.

That's not to say it wouldn't be a hassle if all our possessions got destroyed, and it's not to say that we wouldn't miss some of them. But we'd gotten to a point where we could enjoy our stuff while we had it, and at the same time we wouldn't be devastated if we lost it. That was a big step toward liberation for us.

As it happened, our house didn't burn down. But we saw the evacuation as a good exercise to go through, not only for the uncluttering we ultimately did to simplify our lives, but for releasing our attachment to possessions and achieving a level of inner contentment.

Look around your house and imagine you have thirty minutes to evacuate and the only things you can take with you are what you can fit in the back of your car. What would you take? If you had to start all over again, how would you do it differently?

We don't have to wait for nature to intervene. We can take responsibility for our lives and begin right now, today, to get rid of the things and our attachments to the things that get in the way of our inner peace.

When you get right down to it, it's surprising how little we need to be happy.

During the later stages of finishing this book, I (Philip) found myself temporarily without an office after a fire destroyed much of our university building. During the time the department was displaced, we were forced by circumstances to discover that we could actually do our jobs without the computer networks, faxes, voicemail and e-mail that we had come to rely on.

We had more patience when little matters that once would have seemed important went awry and a new thankfulness when they didn't. We discovered a new appreciation of each other's presence when temporary office arrangements scattered us. There was a new grace in the way that we treated each other and our students. In short, we became more human and more adept at the simple art of teaching.

Jesus taught a similar lesson to his disciples in Matthew 10:9-10 when he sent them out for their first teaching and healing experience. After telling them where to go and what to do once they were there, he told them "not [to] take along any gold or silver or copper in [their] belts; take no bag for the journey, or extra tunic, or sandals or a staff; for the worker is worth his keep." By sending them out without any tangible means of support, Jesus was making sure that they would rely totally on his assurances that he would provide for their needs.

The same challenge is put to us today. We must make the promises of God leap off the pages of our Bibles and into our everyday living. We must try something so bold that if God is not behind it, it will fail. Then and only then will we be able to test his promises and know his will for our lives.

Good luck on your journey. Remember to travel light, and we'll see you at the final destination.

Questions for Thought or Discussion

1. What keeps us from being able to "see our sin"?

2. What has been the greatest cost you have paid to be a Christian?

3. If you had only thirty minutes and the space in the back of your car, what items would you want from your home? Why?

Resources

Books

Albert, Susan Wittig. *Work of Her Own.* New York: G. P. Putnam's Sons, 1992.

Cahn, Edgar, and Jonathan Rowe. *Time Dollars.* Emmaus, Penn.: Rodale, 1991.

Covey, Stephen. *The Seven Habits of Highly Effective Families.* New York: Simon & Schuster, 1997.

———. *The Seven Habits of Highly Effective People.* New York: Simon & Schuster, 1989.

Culp, Stephanie. *Streamlining Your Life: A Five-Point Plan for Uncomplicated Living.* Cincinnati: Writer's Digest Books, 1991.

Dacyczyn, Amy. *The Tightwad Gazette.* New York: Villard, 1993.

Dominguez, Joe, and Vicki Robin. *Your Money or Your Life.* New York: Penguin, 1993.

Elgin, Duane. *Voluntary Simplicity.* New York: Quill, 1993.

Eller, Vernard. *The Simple Life: The Christian Stance Toward Possessions.* Grand Rapids, Mich.: Eerdmans, 1973.

Fassel, Diane. *Working Ourselves to Death.* San Francisco: HarperSanFrancisco, 1990.

Foster, Richard J. *Freedom of Simplicity.* San Francisco: Harper & Row, 1981.

Hewlett, Sylvia. *When the Bough Breaks.* New York: BasicBooks, 1991.

Hochschild, Arlie. *The Second Shift.* New York: Viking, 1989.

———. *The Time Bind: When Work Becomes Home and Home Becomes Work.* New York: Henry Holt, 1997.

Kanter, Rosabeth Moss. *When Giants Learn to Dance.* New York: Simon

& Schuster, 1989.

Keys, Ralph. *Timelock*. New York: HarperCollins, 1991.

Lague, Louise. *The Working Mom's Book of Hints, Tips and Everyday Wisdom*. Princeton, N.J.: Peterson's, 1990.

Lewis, David, Carley Dodd and Darryl Tippens. *The Gospel According to Generation X*. Abilene, Tex.: Abilene Christian University Press, 1995.

McGee-Cooper, Ann. *You Don't Have to Go Home from Work Exhausted!* Dallas: Bowen & Rogers, 1990.

McGovern, George. *Terry: My Daughter's Life-and-Death Struggle with Alcoholism*. New York: Villard, 1996.

Peters, Tom, and Nancy Austin. *A Passion for Excellence*. New York: Random House, 1985.

Rechtschaffen, Stephan. *Time Shifting: Creating More Time to Enjoy Your Life*. New York: Doubleday, 1996.

Robinson, John, and Geoffrey Godbey. *Time for Life*. State College: Pennsylvania State Press, 1995.

St. James, Elaine. *Inner Simplicity*. New York: Hyperion, 1995.

————. *Simplify Your Life*. New York: Hyperion, 1994.

Saltzman, Amy. *Downshifting*. New York: HarperCollins, 1991.

Schor, Juliet P. *The Overworked American*. New York: BasicBooks, 1991.

Shenk, David. *Data Smog*. New York: Harper-Edge, 1997.

Stampi, Claudio. *Why We Nap*. Boston: Birkheauser, 1992.

Swenson, Richard. *Margin*. Colorado Springs, Colo.: NavPress, 1994.

Thurman, Howard. *The Inward Journey*. New York: Harper, 1961.

White, Edward. *A Sense of Presence*. Nashville: Christian Communications, 1989.

Winston, Stephanie. *Stephanie Winston's Best Organizing Tips*. New York: Simon & Schuster, 1996.

Newspapers

Boyd, Danny M. "High Interest? It's in the Cards." *Daily Oklahoman*, October 6, 1996, sec. B, p. 1.

Burney, Teresa. "Bosses Are Learning That Flexibility Builds Loyalty."

St. Petersburg Times, June 28, 1996, sec. G, p. 1.

———. "How Companies Make Room for Families." *St. Petersburg Times,* June 29, 1996, sec. E, pp. 8-11.

———. "Preparing for Vacation Can Wear Workers Out." *St. Petersburg Times,* June 30, 1996, sec. G, p. 1.

Kristol, Irving. "Life Without Father." *The Wall Street Journal.* March 15, 1995, p. A1.

Maney, Kevin. "Information Age Executives Not Hung Up on Sleep." *USA Today,* July 6, 1993, sec. C, p. 1.

Shellenbarger, Sue. "Researchers Say Children Feel Job Stress." *Sarasota Herald-Tribune,* August 1, 1996, sec. D, pp. 1-2.

Magazines

Adler, Jerry. "Kids Growing Up Scared." *Newsweek,* January 10, 1994, pp. 43-50.

Balzer, Harry. "The Ultimate Cooking Appliance." *American Demographics,* July 1993, pp. 40-44.

Bloch, Gordon. "I Don't Have Time." *Runner's World,* January 1991, pp. 32-35.

Collingwood, Harris. "Simplicity Simplified." *Working Woman,* December 1995, pp. 48-50.

Edmondson, Brad. "Do You Have the Tickets?" *American Demographics,* April 1995, pp. 3.

Ehrenreich, Barbara. "In Search of a Simpler Life." *Working Woman,* December 1995, pp. 27-29, 62.

Fisher, Anne B. "Welcome to the Age of Overwork." *Fortune,* November 30, 1992, pp. 64-71.

Flatow, Sheryl. "I Will Not Lose My Family for This Job." *Parade,* July 14, 1996, pp. 15-16.

Gibbs, Nancy. "How America Has Run Out of Time." *Time,* April 24, 1989.

Ingrassia, Michele. "Virgin Cool." *Newsweek,* October 17, 1994, pp. 59-69.

Lehman, Elliott. "Business Must Do More for Working Parents." *Parade,* February 26, 1995, pp. 12-14.

McDonough, David. "Afternoon Delight." *Ambassador,* June 1996, pp. 32-35.

McDowell, Josh. "Study Shows Church Kids Not Waiting." *Christianity Today,* March 18, 1988, pp. 54-55.

O'Reilly, Brian. "Is Your Company Asking Too Much?" *Fortune,* March 12, 1990, pp. 38-46.

Quindlen, Anna. "Why I Quit." *Working Woman,* December 1995, pp. 30-33.

Shapiro, Laura. "The Myth of Quality Time." *Newsweek,* May 12, 1997, pp. 62-69.

Shaw, Elizabeth. "Is This What Life's About?" *Newsweek,* May 5, 1997, p. 22.

Willis, Clint. "How to Afford the Life You Want." *Working Woman,* December 1995, pp. 35-37, 68-70.

Television Programs

Affluenza. Produced by KCTS-TV, Seattle, Washington. Aired by PBS on September 15, 1997.